The Radio Book™

The Complete Station Operations Manual

Volume One:
Management & Sales Management

1995 Edition

Edited by: B. Eric Rhoads
Reed Bunzel
Anne Snook
Wendy McManaman
Vicky Bowles

Cover and Book Designed by:
Practical Graphics, Inc.
2090 Palm Beach Lakes Boulevard, Suite 903
West Palm Beach, Florida 33409

West Palm Beach, Florida

Streamline Press is a division of Streamline Publishing, Inc.

ISBN: 1-886-74500-5 (Vol. #1)
SET: 1-886-74503-X (3 Vol. Set)

Library of Congress Catalog Card Number:
The Radio Book Vol. #1 95-67239

Published by and distributed by:
Streamline Press
224 Datura Street, Suite 718
West Palm Beach, Florida 33401-9601
Phone 407-655-8778
Fax 407-655-6164

Printed in the United States of America

TABLE *of* CONTENTS

TABLE *of* CONTENTS

TABLE *of* CONTENTS

PREFACE

Radio is an ever-changing medium. As members of the Radio community, we must become students of the industry to grow our industry, our station revenues and our personal revenues. That, of course, is easier said than done. Time is a valuable and rare commodity. Nevertheless, without taking the time to invest in our growth, we risk becoming stagnant. Thus we begin to regress gradually. To stay on the cutting edge, we must seek intellectual stimulation.

All too often we tend to believe that "there's nothing new in Radio." Perhaps old ideas do resurface with a new face. However, new ideas can change the way we operate — even if they're old ideas in a new package. This book is filled with ideas: Some are old; others are fresh and new. Even revisiting the basics is important. After all, your circumstances and experiences have changed since you learned the basics. Reveiwing them can give you new ways of applying them or can refresh ideas you've long since forgotten.

We encourage you to use this book as a means of stimulating thought and building a better career, a better station and a better industry. This is not a one-sitting book, but rather a reference book. When you've got a problem, turn to the index and find a chapter relating to your need. You'll find it a valuable tool.

B. Eric Rhoads, Publisher

Chapter 1

What Is Your Management Style?

By Dave Gifford

What makes a great sales manager? Someone — anyone who breaks sales records? Are bottom line results the only criteria? Back in the '60s as a kid general manager without the title (I was the sales manager; we didn't have a GM), we doubled our billing in a single year. We more than doubled our billing in a single year. In spite of my management.

I was a hero, you understand, a company star. I was also one lousy manager. Why? Because my management style at that time might be best characterized as just a little to the right of Genghis Khan or Attila the Hun. Management by fear! Nothing wrong with that, right? It got results, didn't it? Whatever works, right? Wrong!

Managing by fear gets results, make no mistake about it. The problem is that salespeople don't get up in the morning looking forward to walking into a moving propeller, and when they get beat up one time too many, they leave. Period.

Back then maybe I had a legitimate excuse: I didn't know any better. And, as naive as that sounds today, understand that the only role models we had in those days were managers who used fear like a shillelagh. Not only was it the prevailing management style of the day, it was the only management style of the day. There weren't any Tom Peterses or Larry Wilsons running around showing us another way; we had to make those discoveries on our own. So, given that in some respects the Radio business is still a cultural generation behind the rest of the business world, what is the excuse today? There isn't any. None!

Nonetheless, this business is still plagued with too many jerks who continue to beat up their salespeople on a regular basis. Tough guys. Intimidators. Table pounders. Screamers. All they prove to their sales people, every single day, is how immature and insecure they really are.

They ought to be pitied, not praised, the poor saps.

What Is Your Management Style?

For what it's worth, here are the 23 guidelines for people management I recommend to the stations I consult:

1.) Everybody likes to be liked, including sales managers, but you're their boss, not their buddy.

2.) Your management style should be made up of an equal mixture of "positive pressure" and "passionate praise."

3.) You should be "demanding, honest and agonizingly fair."

4.) Your salespeople should respect you first, trust you next and like you last. In fact, if they end up liking you, consider that your real bonus.

5.) Do not ask for loyalty and, no, you cannot earn it, either. There is no such thing as loyalty to a company, a Radio station or to a sales manager.

6.) A "mature" manager is only as tough as he or she has to be.

7.) No destructive memos! A destructive memo is the handmaiden of a coward.

8.) What you want is knee-to knee-communication, adult-to-adult. Everybody should be respected as a human being and treated with respect. The dialogue must be two-way, with everybody knowing where they stand.

9.) Nobody is ever embarrassed in public. Ever!

10.) "All people are created equal ... except salespeople." — Giff. Does that mean you can play favorites? No, it just means that you also need to recognize and manage the differences between people. Different strokes for different folks and, yes, different rules for proven veterans (conditionally) vs. unproved veterans and rookies. Based on their ongoing proven performance and never on their experience (tenure) alone.

11.) Fear of loss, according to the human behaviorists, is a far stronger emotion than desire for gain. Fact: You have to experience a life-shattering experience only once to fully appreciate how fragile the human condition can be. Which means, especially when you think about how many times a Radio salesperson experiences rejection, you have to work on building up each salesperson's self-confidence all the time.

12.) A salesperson's self-image is a reflection of:

- How she or he feels about themselves.
- How their peers feel about them.
- How people they respect feel about them.
- How others feel about them.

The point is that the opinions of those they respect the most are the opinions that count the most. Your opinion! What do your salespeople think about your opinion of them, and how much influence do you think your opinion has on their self-image?

13.) Your relationship with your staff, depending on the issues of the day, can change from day to day. How come? To begin with, the cultural environment inside a Radio station is a very sensitive organism. People outside the business may find it impossible to believe, but relationships inside a Radio station are so sensitive that every conversation you have with a salesperson actually changes your relationship with that salesperson. Every single conversation! Either your well-chosen words serve to improve your relationship, or your not-so-well-chosen words set in motion that relationship's deterioration. And somehow, as sales manager, in order to keep your equilibrium, you have to develop the capacity to keep track of each one of those "last conversations" for instant recall. Lesson: Engage brain before engaging mouth.

14.) Your salespeople have to be made to feel important, as if this is an employee-owned Radio station and each salesperson is making an important personal contribution to this station's success.

15.) Solicit their ideas, their suggestions, their recommendations, their opinions (especially their opinions!) — and even their criticisms and bitches.

16.) When your salespeople need your time (unless you're in the middle of putting out a major fire), drop everything, turn off the phone calls, give them your time and listen.

17.) Listen first, talk last.

18.) Love and support your salespeople. It's amazing how the words "thank you for your help" and "you're doing a great job," when deserved, can help you better manage your salespeople.

19.) Be their cheerleader! Praise publicly, privately and in a follow-up memo. Praise their accomplishments and their progress, naturally, but also praise extraordinary efforts as well as extraordinary successes. Everyone is to be encouraged and helped along the way, so long as they help themselves along the way.

20.) All reprimands must be handled live and privately in one-to-one meetings on Tuesday, Wednesday and Thursday only. Never on a Monday or a Friday. Never start or end someone's week with reprimands.

21.) Whenever you have to take someone apart, it's your responsibility to put them back together in even better shape. Nobody goes home beat up and/or with a knot in their stomach. So, praise first, criticize second, show them how next and pump 'em up last.

22.) Never preach your doubts! Not about your lousy morning man, not about a failing salesperson, not about anything.

23.) Share no confidences! Ben Franklin said it best: "Three people can keep a secret ... if two of them are dead."

It's my conviction that a great sales manager is really a kind of "benevolent dictator." Benevolent in the application of one's people skills. But when it comes to keeping your eyes on the prize — achieving the station's billing goals — a dictator when it comes to how that prize is to be won. You're their boss, not their buddy and, to borrow a copy line from an old Burger King ad, you've got to "have it your way," period. However, if you ever get fired, maybe you're better off getting fired for not properly managing the how, rather than for improperly managing the people who work for you. Why?

In this business it's not unusual for someone to be given a second chance after learning from the mistakes of a previous management failure — a failure to achieve a Radio station's billing goals — but there is nothing more lasting than a reputation for being a sales manager who can't manage people. Beware!

Chapter 2

A Sales Manager's Job Description

Draft Your Own

By Dave Gifford

The place to start this chapter is to provide you with a real-world job description you can use. Real-world in the sense that incomplete job descriptions encourage incomplete jobs, and this one is complete. Think of it as a menu from which to choose in drafting your own.

- **Incomplete job descriptions encourage incomplete jobs.**
- **You will be responsible for planning and organizing the sales department, including staffing, budgets, sales efforts, paperwork, reporting systems, credit approval and collections.**
- **Your goal-setting should include: establishing yearly, quarterly, monthly, weekly and daily goals and increasing your station's billing and cash flow.**
- **Remember that you will also be responsible for goal-getting; monitoring and controlling salespeople and accounts; creating, developing and managing your station's strategies and tactics; analyzing and tracking your competition; activating and training your sales staff.**

Planning & Organization

You will be held responsible for:

1.) Answering to and taking directions from the station's general manager.

2.) Organizing the sales department.

3.) Preparing, for approval, the station's sales budget (to include a cost-effective compensation plan for each salesperson).

4.) Staffing the sales department (recruiting, interviewing, selecting, hiring, keeping, promoting and replacing).

5.) Leading and managing the sales staff.

6.) Developing people who will help you and the station achieve its billing goals and critical sales objectives.

7.) Matching your salespeople to accounts that will yield a maximum return to the station.

8.) Planning the sales effort (short to long term.)

9.) Handling credit approval and collections.

10.) Establishing all procedural, paperwork and reporting systems relating to the sales and sales service function.

11.) Establishing, as "conditions of employment," minimum standards of performance requirement for each salesperson.

12.) Conducting productive exit interviews.

13.) Anticipating and managing "change" and new challenges.

Goal-Setting

You will be held responsible for:

1.) Establishing the station's yearly, quarterly, monthly, weekly and daily billing goals and critical sales objectives, and revising same as appropriate and as approved.

2.) Increasing the station's billing, cash flow, profits and market share by increasing • The number of first-time-ever calls weekly ("opportunity" calls, not "cold" calls) • The number of presentations weekly (presentations, not "calls") • The number of written presentations weekly • The number of demonstration tape (spec spot) presentations weekly • The staff's closing ratio (order to presentations) • The number of orders booked weekly • The dollar amount of the station's average order • The station's average unit rate • The station's average weekly billing • The number of accounts billed monthly • The number of new accounts billed monthly • The station's average monthly billing • The staff's renewal ratio (renewals to original orders) • The staff's collection ratio (percent of monthly accounts receivable).

Goal-Getting

You will be held responsible for:

1.) Committing yourself, personally, to achieving the station's billing goals and critical sales objectives.

2.) Fielding the largest, most self-motivated, most-disciplined, best-trained, best-supported, most constantly activated, most-effective, best-paid Radio sales force in the market.

3.) Establishing specialist sales teams and/or individual specialist assignments as applicable.

4.) Creating, developing and managing the station's "sales format" (strategies & tactics).

5.) Determining the sales priorities, emphasis and activities as circumstances dictate.

6.) Analyzing the market for sales opportunities.

7.) Identifying potential markets (traditional and non-traditional) for new business development.

8.) Analyzing the competition (all) and tracking same on a day-to-day basis.

9.) Developing leads and supervising all prospecting activities.

10.) Developing specified target accounts to maximize their potential.

11.) Selling the station on the basis of "supply and demand" by putting pressure on your inventory via the most aggressive and innovative sales effort in the market.

12.) Creating and developing, on an ongoing basis, a basic sales menu (sponsorships, sales promotions, packages, etc.).

13.) Establishing a minimum order policy.

14.) Developing and managing the use of the station's training and sales tools.

15.) Developing applicable sales presentations.

16.) Providing a high standard of client service.

17.) Assisting in the servicing of the station's key and new accounts.

18.) Assisting in the creation, development and planning of the station's advertising and promotional efforts.

19.) Arranging approved trades and ticket, prize and dub pickups, etc.

20.) Maximizing the station's competitive advantages (favorable ratings, qualitative research, success stories, value-added services, etc.).

21.) Supervising the preparation of all collateral materials (media kit, one sheets, etc.).

22.) Representing the station in activities within the advertising and business communities.

23.) Personally positioning the station's vital importance to the market's largest advertisers and agencies.

24.) Maximizing your time management for maximum effectiveness.

25.) Pursuing your own personal management development program.

26.) Creating, developing and evaluating new programs, systems and ideas as advisable.

Controlling

You will be held responsible for:

1.) Monitoring and controlling, on an ongoing basis, all costs against the annual sales budget.

2.) Collecting, on a monthly basis, 55 percent of the station's accounts receivable.

3.) Establishing an official rate negotiation strategy formulated to increase the station's average unit rate.

4.) Managing the inventory to maximize station billing.

5.) Charting the progress of the sales effort on a day-to-day basis.

6.) Reporting, on a monthly basis, the station's sales performance against preset budget goals.

7.) Charting the progress of individual salespeople against preset minimum standards of performance.

8.) Evaluating their in-field performances.

9.) Reporting, on a monthly basis, individual sales performances.

10.) Monitoring, on an ongoing basis, all competitive advertising sales activity.

11.) Attending all meetings where your presence is necessary.

12.) Coordinating, with other department heads, all sales functions that cross over into their departmental responsibilities.

13.) Reviewing, for modification or abandonment, all station sales activities, policies and procedures, on an ongoing basis.

14.) Keeping all parties informed, as appropriate, of any and all changes and modifications.

15.) Establishing a network of feedback resources (clients, competitors, agencies, etc.) that may be useful in helping you make timely decisions.

16.) Getting to the center of problems quickly and solving same quickly.

17.) Developing your salespeople as "self" managers.

18.) Resolving, in a mutually satisfactory manner, all conflicts relating to the sales function.

19.) "Turning" complacent, slumping, failing and problem salespeople.

20.) Planning and conducting all sales meetings.

21.) Delegating assignments and tasks as appropriate. Includes delegating decision-making authority where appropriate.

22.) Keeping your national and/or regional sales representatives informed.

23.) Measuring the long-term impact of all your decisions.

Activation (Not "Motivation")

You will be held responsible for:

1.) Activating the sales staff to achieve all station and individual billing goals and critical sales objectives.

2.) Being "demanding, honest and agonizingly fair" in your day-to-day supervision of the sales staff.

3.) Listening to your salespeople's ideas, suggestions, recommendations, opinions, criticisms and bitches, and encouraging their input into your decision-making.

4.) Building the salespeople's self-confidence through positive reinforcement.

5.) Providing one-on-one help and guidance to each salesperson on a weekly basis.

6.) Developing and maintaining an enthusiastic and positive "team esteem" pride in the company, the station and its sales effort.

7.) Establishing high ethical standards.

8.) Managing, by example, by assisting the salespeople in the field.

9.) Managing, by example, by successfully covering a small but important list of your own accounts.

10). Disciplining, as appropriate, when discipline is appropriate.

11). Firing anyone, with just cause (documented), who stands in your way of achieving the station's billing goals and critical sales objectives.

12.) Developing a successor.

Training (Counseling/Coaching/Correcting/Developing)

You will be held responsible for determining the sales staff's critical training needs and identifying the skill deficiencies of each salesperson. You will be held responsible for improving those performance requirements (see "Goal-Setting") that will have the most impact on achieving the station's billing goals. You will be held responsible for getting the salespeople to focus on:

1.) Making more presentations.
2.) Getting their "unfair" share of business (larger orders).
3.) Getting more new business.
4.) Getting more long-term business.
5.) "Upsetting" current clients.
6.) Getting more co-op and vendor sales.
7.) Selling the agencies vertically and between the buys.
8.) Selling creatively.
9.) Getting results for advertisers.
10.) Making collections.
11.) Taking more risks.
12.) Becoming more assertive.
13.) Working harder.
14.) Working smarter.

You will be held responsible for improving their:

1.) Organization.
2.) Overall planning.
3.) Pre-call planning.
4.) Follow-through.
5.) Paperwork and record-keeping.

6.) Computer skills (as applicable).
7.) Time and travel management.
8.) Territory management (if applicable).
9.) Account management.
10.) Prospecting.
11.) Qualifying.
12.) Analytical skills.
13.) Problem-solving skills.
14.) Customer service.
15.) Overall selling skills.
16.) Specific selling skills.

You will be held responsible for teaching them:

1.) The fundamentals of Radio programming.
2.) Copywriting & commercial production techniques.
3.) Competitive media essentials.
4.) Marketing essentials.
5.) Distribution essentials.
6.) Advertising essentials.
7.) Reach & frequency essentials (OES).
8.) Sales promotion essentials.
9.) Ad agency essentials.
10.) Retailing essentials.
11.) Co-op essentials.
12.) Vendor sales essentials.

Chapter 3

Good, Clean Sound

Making Your Station Sound Better

By Roy Pressman

Historical or Hysterical? "The louder the station, the higher the ratings?" In the 1970s, FM Radio took off. FM sounded better than AM, and listeners noticed the difference. A lot of theories that applied to AM Radio carried over to FM and were simply not valid. One theory, "the louder the station, the higher the ratings," seems to linger on. Loudness has nothing to do with the coverage contours of an FM station, and I have yet to see a study proving otherwise.

The "louder the better" theory is still strong in the minds of many programmers and managers. You can clearly see that equipment manufacturers have reacted to this belief and continue to manufacture processing that is reaching the theoretical limits of loudness. Fortunately, most of this equipment, when adjusted properly, can be loud and clean at the same time. It wasn't possible in the '70s.

Wish List

"I want it louder, cleaner, brighter, better bass, less noise, more highs, more separation ... than the competition!"

Sounds like a wish, all right! 1) Try to be competitively loud, but remember loudness isn't everything. 2) Keep the distortion and clipping to a minimum to achieve long listening times (minimizing clipping and distortion can reduce station loudness). 3) Don't go crazy with the equalization. The music you play on the air should approximate what comes off the LP or CD. 4) Use compression and limiting in moderation. (Compression reduces the dynamic range of the station, and limiting controls the program material peaks and prevents overmodulation ... high levels of limiting and compression can contribute to listener fatigue.)

Give your listeners' ears a break! Compromise is the best solution to shaping the sound of any Radio station. There is a trade-off between loudness and reduced distortion. Careful listening will tell you what combination is right for your station.

Department Of Redundancy

"Yes, we have all the latest processing equipment on the air now." Don't fall into the trap of trying to use too many compressor/processors at once. Justify the use of each piece of equipment in your processing chain. Use just enough processing to get the job done. Remember, the less equipment the signal has to go through, the better your station is going to sound. The shortest path between your studio and your listeners' ears is usually the best.

Stop, Look And Listen

Audio processing is more like cooking than science. You may not understand manufacturers' specifications, but you own the most sensitive instruments in the world: your ears. Take time to develop your listening skills. Always listen to your station on at least three different types of receivers (clock Radio, car Radio and home stereo). Listen to your competition. If you need to make changes to your on-air sound, make them gradually so you don't lose your frame of reference. Don't play with the processing. Find the combination that works well for you, and then leave the dials alone. The right combination of ingredients results in a clean, competitive sound that will give your station that winning edge.

Garbage In, Garbage Out

Replace old studio equipment before spending thousands of dollars on audio processing. Start with good studios that have up-to-date equipment. Make sure the studios are wired properly and, yes, neatness counts. If what comes out of your studios is clean (it should sound as good or better than your home stereo), then you're way ahead of the game. If your facility is old, you may want to consider replacing studio equipment before spending thousands of dollars on a new processor. Audio processing is not the way to correct your studio deficiencies. When you feed clean audio into your audio processing equipment, you'll be surprised how easy it is to achieve a good on-air sound.

Chapter 4

How Men See Women In Radio

Get To The Point!

By Gina Gallagher

The '90s present new challenges for both men and women. We have been in the throes of a gender-bending era. The roles of men and women have seemingly homogenized — women have become stronger and men have become more sensitive. This role change has transformed the corporate culture to include more women in the workplace. The number of women in sales and management in some cases outnumbers the males.

- **Women spend too much time on details; they don't focus on the end result.**
- **Men want to control their own destinies, and women feel the need to be in charge — this is a potential clash.**
- **Male bosses are more like coaches; female bosses are more nurturing.**
- **Women try too hard to be supportive.**

How are women in Radio viewed by their male counterparts? Following are excerpts from candid conversations with Bob, 38 and married, Alan, 35 and single, and Ray, 36 and married — all of whom have worked for a woman in Radio.

Do You Think Women Have A Different Approach To Work Than Men?

Bob: Women spend too much time on relationships and don't get to the point as quickly as men.

Alan: Women work hard, sometimes harder than men. The problem is they spend too much time on the details. They obsess on getting one small thing right. They don't focus on the end result. They are concerned with the process, and they want it done their way.

Ray: They are compulsive about being the best and taking care of everything. Sometimes I feel as if I am in school. (I wish that they would) just tell me the result (they) are looking for and let me get my job done. If I need input, I'll ask for it. Respect my competence. Don't treat me like I am one of your kids.

Do Women Get Down To Business Fast Enough?

Bob: We can generalize all day about men and women. It's all a matter of style. Some men try building rapport with insincere chatter, and so do some women. Some people are more focused and have the skills that balance rapport and business.

Alan: Once again, I feel that women tend to be more relationship-oriented and more verbal than men. Sometimes I feel it's more important for me to agree with my boss; otherwise, she will continue to press me and won't be satisfied until I tell her she's right — even if I have another view. Now I know why my dad always said "yes, dear" to my mom ... it just wasn't worth the fight.

Ray: No, our meetings go all over the place. Sometimes they become lectures, but this has also been the case with some of the male sales managers. My current manager takes an hour to deal with something that could just as easily have been addressed in a memo.

What Is It Like To Work For A Female Manager?

Bob: Some women will be great managers; others won't. Women have to relate differently to the male psyche. Men need to feel that they are still in charge of their own destiny, and if women need to feel in charge (too), there will be a real contest.

Alan: I like working with women, but it's harder than working for a guy. I feel freer in my interactions with a man. I think a guy tends to be more concerned with the end result and he will let you figure out how to get there. I think a guy is more of a coach and a woman tends to be more of a nurturer who can't let go and trust the process.

Ray: I have to say I've worked for two women and it gets a little too touchy-feely for me. I don't like feeling I'm being given a performance appraisal by my mother. Get to the point; tell me in what areas you'd like to see improvement and quit trying to get me to feel.

Do You Think Women Try Too Hard To Be Tough-Minded?

Bob: They try too hard to be supportive. What gets me is when female managers patronize you before they let you have it; the compliment followed by "but ... I" feels like it's one big manipulation.

Alan: I think women have great organizational skills and the know-how to get things done. Personally, I get along great (with them). I just tell her what she wants to hear and then I concentrate on doing a great job. You have to play games no matter what sex you are working for.

Ray: I get the feeling that my manager is trying too hard at being in control. She thinks that she has to be on top of everything. She really is a great person and has good intentions, but she tends to get real defensive if you don't agree with her. So I just tell her what she wants to hear.

Draw conclusions about your own interactions with your male counterparts, ladies, and remember that the true meaning of your communications is the response you get. The only things you can control are your own actions and reactions.

Chapter 5

Remotivate Burned-Out Salespeople

. . . Before It's Too Late

By Pam Lontos

- **Be aware of changes in salespeople's energy levels.**
- **Burnout has three components: physical, emotional and mental exhaustion. Exhaustion in one area leads to a temporary slump; in all three, to burnout.**
- **Managers must identify burnout warning signs early and help salespeople regain balance in their lives, find out what's needed to get them remotivated and provide positive reinforcement.**

Something awful can happen if you are out of touch with your topmost salespeople. They can burn out.

Low-performance salespeople don't put enough stress on themselves to burn out. To burn out, a person needs to have been on fire. Low performers may just be demotivated, lazy or bored, and a new goal or management can quickly get them back on track and producing.

Burned-out salespeople are beyond that. They're like a house that has suffered an out-of-control fire and is burning to the ground. Nothing but ashes will remain if the danger goes unnoticed for too long, and it will require much more than a simple touch-up or a new paint job to bring it back.

Burnout can be devastating to your Radio station. It's difficult enough to find good salespeople without losing those who are contributing to your success. You can't afford to let this happen. If it does, you must do everything you can to save them.

Early Warning Signs

Be aware of changes in your salespeople's energy levels. Sales performance may still be good, but the same high energy level — the sparkle in the eyes — will be missing. Life or work is just not enjoyable anymore.

Often, managers tend to dismiss this sign because it hasn't shown up dramatically in sales figures. Then, when their salespeople's sales start to slump, they think it's temporary. They ignore it or provide some minimal motivation while waiting for the fire and high sales to return.

They do this because it has worked before. But when it doesn't work, their burned-out salespeople may either leave or have to be let go. Net profit will suffer either way. Avoid letting your top salespeople get into such a deep depression that they can't get out. Learn the difference between burnout and a temporary slump.

Burnout Vs. Temporary Slump

Burnout has three basic components: physical, mental and emotional exhaustion. Exhaustion in one area leads to a slump; in all three, to burnout. Burned-out employees can not be rekindled overnight.

If your salespeople are physically exhausted (from working or playing too hard), extra rest will recharge them.

If they suffer from emotional exhaustion (often the result of relationship problems), helping them solve the problem or just letting them talk about it can get them back on the road to success.

If your salespeople are mentally exhausted (from a negative attitude toward life, work and self), they need help in becoming more positive to get their energy back.

Since burnout means physical, emotional and mental capacities are all depleted, managers must work on all three areas.

Balance And Motivation

We are thrilled when someone constantly overworks and overproduces. However, it won't last forever unless that person is able to recharge. People often overwork to avoid problems elsewhere. Their lives are out of balance. Managers must help them get their lives back in sync so it isn't all work and no play.

Brian Tracy, a leading speaker on human potential, asks in his seminars: "How would you spend your life if you knew you had only six months to live, and how is your current life consistent with that?" If your salespeople are leaving important things in their lives out, help them get them back. They will become more enthused and be able to sell more with less work.

When people are out of balance, they subject themselves to high stress and low performance. Low stress and higher performance exist when all parts of one's life are in harmony.

Tracy says: "We all need motivation. Motivation requires a motive. A vital function of management is to produce appropriate motivation to people to perform at their best.

"If a person is in a slump, it means they have no clear motivation for action. People are motivated for their reasons, not ours. A manager's job is to help discover or rediscover what motivated the employee in the past and encourage them to believe they can achieve it again." Find out their dreams and help them achieve them.

John Rockweiler, vice president and general manager of V103.9, Los Angeles, also subscribes to this approach: " ... sit down with the salesperson and review their poor performance. Relate it to burnout. Issue a challenge. Give them definite performance standards to achieve over a time period, 30 or 60 days. Make the standard very achievable. Let them rediscover the feeling of winning, of achieving and accomplishing goals."

Peggy Neer, sales manager of Country 103, South Bend, Indiana, concurs. "You need to know what motivates each person on the sales staff. It's usually something different for each person. Maybe the salesperson needs a new and exciting challenge — something to get the energy flowing again."

Neer also recommends going with the salesperson on sales calls. "Let them know you care about them, not only professionally but also as a person. Reinforce the fact that you are behind them and supportive. Let them know you are willing to spend time with them daily to get them back on track."

Zig Ziglar, sales trainer, author and motivational teacher, says: " ... the manager must understand that the seeds of greatness do exist in every human being, including that burned-out employee ... he should repeatedly understand and remind that employee that failure is an event ... not a person, that yesterday really did end last night ... the manager should remind the employee that attitude is entirely a matter of choice and he chooses his attitude when he chooses the input into his mind, and so he should choose daily to read and listen to positive materials, and, to the full extent of his ability, associate with positive individuals."

When Lisa Hester of KJNO, Juneau, Alaska, sees her salespeople approaching burnout, she has them change their thinking. "Refocus your goals to a more positive association, such as your dream house or a vacation vs. a dollar quota."

Positive Reinforcement

A primary way to promote feelings of growth and possessiveness is with sales and motivational programs provided by management. I constantly recommend tapes and books to salespeople who get in a slump and need positive reinforcement to counteract the daily rejection and hard work that lead high achievers toward burnout.

Burnout is a tragedy because it ruins your top performers. Highly motivated people don't work hard just because of money. They identify with their work and want recognition and appreciation. Managers who want to keep their top salespeople must constantly praise, notice and encourage them. Don't give all the attention to the low achievers, thinking that the high achievers are a gravy train that will last forever.

People are not machines. Stress wears them out by lowering the production of norepinephrine and endorphins, which activate the reward center of the brain. When the tissues producing these chemicals are fatigued, people become depressed and unproductive.

Watch for overwork. Tell people when they need to slow down, or take a vacation or long weekend.

Exercise helps restore positive endorphins to the body. Often, salespeople in a slump become inactive, furthering the depression. Encourage them to get into an exercise program. This is a different activity from their work. This releases endorphins and lifts their spirits.

Let salespeople talk with you about their frustrations, anger and problems. Holding in these emotions leads to fatigue, depression and lost sales.

Help salespeople realize that "this too shall pass." They must not get into a mode of thinking that they will never sell again. They must realize that, with a little effort on their part and support from management, the slump will disappear and they again will bring in those large orders.

Encourage them to temporarily lower their own demands. Slow down, recharge. Relaxation exercises, deep breathing, meditation or taking a quiet walk to relieve stress can get them back to normal.

A house that is burning can be saved if the fire is caught early. Burnout is less likely to happen or will be less devastating if we are aware of its approach. Watch for the early warning signs and step in to support, educate and help "troubled" employees change their ways before it's too late.

Chapter 6

Ride 'N' Ignore The Ratings

The Optimum Moneymaking Strategy

By Rick Ott

A Radio station can adopt two traditional moneymaking strategies today: One that depends on ratings, and the other that de-emphasizes the ratings. A third strategy, actually a combination of the first two, is gaining in popularity. Take a look at each, and see which might be your best option.

- **Traditional moneymaking strategies include trumpeting your higher-than-the-competition ratings or ignoring your not-so-great "book" performance altogether.**
- **The strongest moneymaking strategy in operation today is a combination of both — doing everything it takes to earn significantly higher ratings, while developing strong local sales departments that do not depend on the numbers at all.**
- **Putting it into effect requires top management adoption and commitment.**

Traditional Strategy No. 1:
Ride The Ratings

Premise: The higher your ratings, especially in "desirable" demo cells like adults 25-54, the more demand there will be for your air time. And high demand results in more time sold at higher rates.

Why this strategy works: The price of anything — air time included — is ultimately controlled by the law of supply and demand. To create demand, broadcasters have learned to limit supply in two ways: First, by garnering higher ratings than competitors, a station sets itself apart, effectively reducing the competitors to less-than-desirable alternatives. Second, by reducing the number of commercial availabilities per hour, the value of each remaining availability increases.

Drawbacks: There are three drawbacks to the Ride The Ratings strategy. First, and most obvious, you must have high ratings for it to work. In fact, you need not only high ratings, but significantly higher ratings than your closest competitor. As we all know, that is not an easy proposition. Second, building and maintaining high ratings is usually a rather expensive undertaking. You've got to spend liberally on programming and especially on marketing (advertising, promotion and contesting) to pull it off. Third, when you live by the ratings sword, you die by the ratings sword. Predicating your success on the numbers is a very precarious position to adopt.

Traditional Strategy No. 2:
Ignore The Ratings

Premise: Advertisers want one thing from Radio: Results. If a station can produce results, through any combination of air time, value-added promotions, vendor programs or whatever, who cares what the station's ratings are? Stations with ratings no better than the competition's ratings have found they can bring in respectable revenue regardless by concentrating on direct sales to results-hungry clients, and by de-emphasizing the numbers.

Why this strategy works: The ratings aren't what they used to be. Due to increased fragmentation, more and more stations end up "bunched together" with ratings so close to one another that the difference between them is insignificant. There's no point in brandishing the ratings book if your numbers are not much different from the other guy's. In fact, ad agencies, who do buy the numbers, find one station just as good as the next these days. Since there's no such thing as any one station being a "must buy" anymore, a station's ability to raise rates based on the numbers has been negated (at the agency level, at least).

Drawbacks: This strategy works only when there is little ratings disparity among stations. And that can change at any time. If and when one station should mount a "pack-breaking" push and surge significantly ahead, the guys left behind will suffer. In that sense, the Ignore The Ratings strategy is a default strategy that becomes effective only when no station in a market (or perhaps only one or two stations in larger markets) operates successfully as a ratings rider. Ratings ignorers remain vulnerable to instant obsolescence of their strategy any time enough competitors decide to step forward and blow it up.

Emerging Strategy: Ride 'N' Ignore The Ratings

The Ride The Ratings and Ignore The Ratings strategies are converging. An increasing number of stations are adopting a strategy that combines the best elements of both.

Ride 'N' Ignore stations are doing what it takes to earn significantly higher ratings. Despite the recession, they continue to spend on programming and marketing. They aggressively flash the ratings to interested buyers, in whatever configuration shows them in best light, to get a buy.

At the same time, they're developing strong local sales departments that do not depend on the numbers at all. These local sales reps talk results — the "bodies-in-building, cash-register-ringing" language that local clients eat up. Most of the time, they never even mention the ratings.

By Riding 'N' Ignoring, a station gains the advantages of both ratings riders and ratings ignorers. And, many of the disadvantages of riding or ignoring cancel out (if the ratings should drop, for example, the local sales department continues to do what it always has, virtually unaffected).

The Ride 'N' Ignore strategy is by far the strongest moneymaking strategy in operation today. Putting it into effect is more than a simple sales decision, however. It's a corporate strategy that must be adopted, and committed to, by top management.

Chapter 7

Better To Pay A Little Now

How Listening To Your Engineer Can Save Money

By Ann Gallagher

Engineering usually comes under the category of overhead, and as such is vulnerable to budget cuts, particularly in the present Radio climate. Many GMs wonder why they should listen to the chief engineer who is telling them the AM station's ground system needs to be replaced, or why they should pay a consulting engineer to help them select a transmitter site.

- **Fixing something once can be much cheaper than constant maintenance.**
- **Planning to side-mount an FM antenna? A pattern study may be indicated.**
- **It can pay to spend a little for coverage studies before you decide where to put your antenna.**
- **Properly managed, excess tower capacity can be very profitable.**

The answer is that some judicious investment in sound engineering can save you money in the long-run. Here are some examples of the sorts of false economies that can make a manager wring his hands and wish he had spent a little for the proverbial ounce of prevention.

One-Time Fix Vs. Constant Maintenance

A few years ago, a chief engineer told his GM that the AM towers needed new ground systems, which would have cost approximately $35,000 at the time. The manager decided the AM wasn't worth the investment. Six years later, when the station sold the land out from under the AM at a substantial profit, the GM told the chief engineer that he was glad he hadn't spent the money for a new ground system at a site they eventually vacated. Was this a good decision? Not really. Without the new ground system, the AM array was unstable. Antenna parameters and monitor point limits tended to exceed FCC-specified limits, and keeping the unstable AM array legal had occupied an engineering type almost full time. The $35,000 was eaten up several times over in extra maintenance costs.

Pattern Studies Can Be Critical

Range testing a nondirectional FM antenna which will be mounted on the side of a tower costs in the neighborhood of $10,000, and is an expense many owners or managers may be tempted to eliminate when faced with high construction costs. Considering how much side-mounting can distort an antenna pattern, particularly on larger-face towers, this is truly a false economy. Pattern distortion can mean that less than half a station's power is directed over the critical market. Judicious placement, on the other hand, can enhance coverage. After all, you have only one thing to sell: your signal.

Shadowing Studies — Cheap Insurance

Every FM application submitted to the FCC contains a coverage map, but these maps may have limited real-world use, especially in rugged terrain. If you are trying to cover a city in a river valley which lies 15 miles from the area where your transmitter site must be, it may be wise to spend some money on terrain-limited coverage studies. These studies can identify areas which would be "shadowed" from a particular antenna location, and can be invaluable in selecting the optimum antenna site and tower height. Spending $1,000 or less on terrain-limited coverage studies can help you avoid the unpleasant surprise of discovering, for example, that a ridge just outside of town destroys your signal in the downtown business district.

Leasing Excess Tower Capacity

Tower construction is another area in which an investment in sound engineering advice can pay — handsomely. An expert in this field is Garr Johnson, director of engineering for the Central Virginia Educational Television Corporation. Johnson's group plans to put up two new towers to support microwave antennas. In each case, Johnson says, "a 200-foot tower would do it, but we're building a 400-foot tower." The group plans to lease excess tower space to two-way and other communication users.

Management was convinced by Johnson's research and experience in the area, which indicated that the cost of a 400-foot tower strong enough to support multiple antennas could be recouped within five years. Not every broadcasting tower is in an area with this kind of revenue potential, of course. Furthermore, Johnson warns, "towers are extremely complex devices to manage." Issues such as frequency compatibility among tenants make it imperative to have an experienced engineer associated with a multiple-antenna site. A properly managed tower, however, can pay for itself within a few years and continue to generate revenue thereafter.

This is not to say that every piece of advice from an engineer makes good business sense. There may be plenty of times when your chief engineer really should repair an old but serviceable piece of equipment. But then again, there are times when it can pay to listen to what the dweeb with the pocket protector is trying to tell you.

Chapter 8

Men And Women: Can We Talk?

The Art Of Powerspeak

By Mimi Donaldson

Mother always told you men and women were different. But just how different? Women tend to take in a number of impressions simultaneously and only later focus on specifics. Men, on the other hand, usually start by focusing on specific facts or physical reality, then move outward to encompass the big picture. The result is that the sexes often drive each other crazy, with men complaining that "women are not focused," while women moan that "men are not flexible." Different views lead to problems. Men like their communications short, to the point and factual. Women tend to be more wordy.

After 19 years of training managers in better communication skills, I have come up with the "Seven Deadly Sins" — the things that drive men crazy and rob women of power.

The "Seven Deadly Sins"

Hedging — Using "kind of," "sort of" and other qualifiers so you don't have to risk responsibility for your ideas and opinions.

Prefacing — Leading into a statement with a phrase that weakens it. For example, "I'm not sure, but ..." or "Can I ask a question?"

Tagging — Adding a qualifying phrase at the end of a statement. Sample: "We should take action, don't you think?"

Filling the silences — women tend to be afraid of silences. They fill them in with non-words, like "um," rather than using them to give power to their statements or opinions.

Cluttering — Using a lot of unnecessary words and phrases that add nothing to communication.

Trying — Saying "I'll try" rather than "I'll do." "Trying" is not the same as "doing."

Smiling and nodding while speaking — Studies have shown that smiling and nodding detract from authority. No one wants to give the big project to a bobbing "kewpie doll."

Overcoming the "Seven Deadly Sins" will give you more power and authority in business situations. And since, like it or not, the power positions in Radio are still dominated by men, it can only be to our benefit!

Chapter 9

You Can't Save Time

The Ten Commandments Of Time Management

By Jack M. Rattigan

Time management and planning. We forfeit so much time and so many sales because we don't manage our time effectively. The person who is organized and plans is on the road to success.

Be The Captain Of Your Ship

We know that ship captains have to file a course plan. They have a destination, a direction and an estimated time of arrival, and have studied the course and possible interventions. They also know that the plan may have to be altered, but they do have a plan. Simple facts. Yet why is it that even though our salespeople desire to "whip the world," they have no idea how they are going to do it or where to start? Successful people do what they plan to do. "Plan your work — work your plan; Fail to plan — plan to fail" ... old cliches but words to live by.

Pocket Planners, Desk Planners, Analyzing Your Options

How do we stop wasting time? Get organized. Prepare a written agenda. Get a pocket planner and carry it with you at

Time Management's Ten Commandments:

1. **Write down your agenda.**
2. **Plan your work — work your plan.**
3. **Be flexible.**
4. **Get organized. Carry a pocket planner for brief notes and dates; keep a desk calendar for exact times and details.**
5. **Categorize your objectives. Is it a "must do"? A "should do"? Or a "nice to do"? The must do's come first.**
6. **Focus on the Good P's — planning, priorities, preparation and presentation. Avoid the bad P — procrastination.**
7. **Get your priorities straight. Set your attention on activities that lead you to your goal.**
8. **Distinguish between important and urgent. Important**

continued

all times. Get a desk planner. Keep it handy and instantly available at your desk. In the pocket planner, list brief notes and times; in the desk planner list more details. Make certain you compare your pocket planner and desk planner daily. (You don't want to commit yourself to being at two different places at the same time.)

Successful time management begins when you analyze your options. Ask yourself into which category a project falls? Is it a "must do"? A "should do"? A "nice to do"? Do the "must do's" first, the "should do's" next and the "nice to do's" only when all else is done.

Planning means setting priorities. What is it you want to accomplish? Keep your mind on the activities that will help you accomplish your goal. The more an activity moves you toward your objective, the higher its priority. Be careful to distinguish "important things" from "urgent things." Important things will lead you to your goal. Urgent things are what you perceive need to be done now. They are not always important. When you are tempted to alter your plan, ask: "Is this going to help me reach my objective?" Stick to your priorities rather than responding to pressure.

What, And When To Do What

A plan tells you what to do; a schedule tells you when to do it. A written itinerary is essential. Salespeople spend time preparing proposals, doing research, picking up copy, traveling, attending meetings, etc. (all necessary), but the only time they are selling is when they are "eyeball-to-eyeball" with the client. Priority must be given to spending more time in selling situations. One of the great time-wasters is driving from call to call, especially from one end of town to the other and then back again. I suggest that salespeople take what I refer to as the "Federal Express" approach. Have them follow a Federal Express truck for an hour. They will quickly learn that the driver has a planned route. There is no "running around town."

Weekly and daily planning are essential. Everyone should plan a daily agenda. Prepare an hour-by-hour schedule a day in advance. Review it before the day begins. Compare the "planned day" with the "actual day" at day's end. Carry over important calls and activities not accomplished to the next day. If this is done every day, good habits will develop.

Divide sales activities so that your salespeople spend half their time with that 20 percent of the clients who represent 80 percent of your business, one-fourth of the time "up-selling" smaller clients and the remaining one-fourth of the time on prospecting for new business. The old standard rule — salespeople should get an early start and not be in the office between 9 a.m. and 4 p.m. — still spells success. Show me a salesperson who spends those hours in the station and I will show you an underachiever.

Throw A Paperwork Party

To all that paperwork — read it, react to it, refer it to someone who can profit from it or trash it. Files? Same thing. Several times a year have a "when in doubt — throw it out party." Announce it a week in advance: "Next Friday at 3 p.m., we are having a party. Bring your jeans and be ready for a fun afternoon." Everyone takes part: sales, programming, promotion, engineering, administration, etc. Everyone is given a garbage bag and told to go through all the junk on the desk, the stuff in the desk drawers and absolutely the files. You won't believe how much trash will disappear. Then send out for pizza and have a party. What does this have to do with time management? Stop to think of all the time wasted looking for important items because there is so much junk you need to go through before you find what you really need.

continued

things lead to your goal.

9. **Control paperwork and files. Read them, react to them, refer them to someone who can benefit from them or trash them. When in doubt, throw it out.**
10. **Spend time wisely.**

No matter how well you plan — be prepared for adjustments. Remember to reward yourself and your staff when you accomplish your goals. There are 8,640 seconds in a day. We must make more of each second. You can't save time — you spend time. Plan to spend it wisely.

Chapter 10

Going Digital

Now Or Later?

By Roy Pressman

The question is not why, but when to purchase digital systems for audio storage and playback.

Digital storage has many advantages over the standard cart machine. However, your decision to switch to digital should not be a hasty one.

Usually, all new products must go through a debugging process. When you purchase this new technology, you could become an unpaid participant in the process. The longer a digital system is on the market, however, the more likely it is to be bug-free.

- **The longer a digital system is on the market, the more likely it is to be bug-free.**
- **Be very careful which system you choose or you could end up with your own digital dinosaur.**
- **Cart machines need constant maintenance, wear out and degrade with every playback.**
- **The advantages of digital: No noise, no distortion, unlimited plays without degradation, instant access to any commercial, almost maintenance-free and no bulky cart storage.**
- **When purchasing a digital storage system, make sure there is a fully redundant system for backup.**
- **Old cart machines can have other uses, so don't abandon them entirely.**

Beware Of Digital Dinosaurs

Each week, more and more companies jump on the digital storage bandwagon. Some systems have more features than others, and prices vary greatly. When the dust settles in a few years, many of these companies will be long gone. Be very careful which digital system and manufacturer you choose today, because you could end up with your own digital dinosaur tomorrow. It will take a few years to see where this is all going, so be patient … if you can. In the meantime, consider this comparison of the two systems.

Analog: Reliable But High-Maintenance

For the past 20 years, broadcasters have used cart machines (analog audio) for playback of commercials and music. Before the advent of the cart machine, commercials were played back via reel-to-reel machines. The on-air personality had to thread the tape, manually cue it and then rewind it.

The cart machine solved these inconveniences and has been proven reliable and functional. However, it brought along its own problems.

Cart machines need constant maintenance. Carts must be bulk-erased before they can be used. And the irregularities of each cart usually cause phase (time delay) problems.

Cart libraries also require a substantial continuous investment. As old carts wear out, new ones must be purchased. (Average cart price $4 each.)

Every time you play back a cart, the quality is slightly degraded. Different tape manufacturer's formulations give different results.

Equipment manufacturers have made a concerted effort over the last 10 years to solve most of the cart machine's problems. We now have reliable cart machines that erase, locate splices and adjust for phase problems automatically. New tape formulations give carts more plays with less degradation of quality.

The Future Is Digital

Digital storage systems overcome the cart machine's inadequacies, plus much more.

The new generation of digital storage devices has not only overcome all of the cart machine's problems, it has surpassed reel-to-reel specifications. No noise, no distortion, unlimited plays without degradation, instant access to any commercial, almost maintenance-free and no bulky cart storage. Computer-based systems and digital cart machines are starting to pop up all over the place.

Digital storage seems too good to be true, but there are some limitations. Most digital storage systems require extremely large hard disk drives just to store the station's commercial library. Usually, CDs are played directly on the air to avoid using up large amounts of disk drive space.

Don't put all your eggs in one basket, though. When purchasing a digital storage system, make sure there is a fully redundant system for backup. How'd you like to have your entire commercial library disappear because of a blip from the power company?

Old Carts, New Tricks

Don't let those old cart machines sit around and collect dust. Each cart machine is a potential income center. By using a cart machine/telephone interface (available from ITC, Harris Allied and others), you can turn any cart machine into an income center. It could be a concert line, job line, weather line — the possibilities are limitless. These information services can be sold to clients or used as an added-value to an advertising schedule.

Chapter 11

How To Select A Consultant

By Rhody Bosley

Life can get very complicated in today's highly competitive Radio environment. The consolidation of ownership, with its subsequent revision of programming and sales goals, makes it all the more interesting. Many managers are finding that the decision-making process requires more information and more points of view.

- **What kind of consultant do you need? What kind of problem do you have?**
- **Have specific, objective goals.**
- **List prospective consultants, consult peers within the industry and prepare questions for the experts you consider hiring.**
- **In addition to determining an expert's cost structure and availability, find out what they expect from you and how they like to work.**
- **Verify expertise with other clients, and prepare a written contract.**

The decision often becomes easier and the results more productive when an outside person or company lends perspective. An outside consultant has the emotional distance to be more objective or the experience to shorten the decision cycle.

There are many jokes about consultants, like: They use your watch to tell you what time it is. And you might like this one: You know who grows up to be a consultant? The kid who used to hold your coat while you fought the schoolyard bully.

Despite all the jokes, the Radio industry supports many consultants for programming, sales, promotion, management, engineering, law and research. The aggregate fees paid are nothing to joke about. However, a consultant's knowledge and experience can save you time lost in going down a non-productive path.

Consultant Selection Guidelines

Here are some guidelines for getting the most out of a consultant's expertise.

1.) The first business decision is what kind of consultant is needed. Is it a programming problem, a personnel problem, a promotion problem, a research problem, etc.? Be careful: Are you the problem? Frankly, the answers are not always clear. Sometimes the experienced consultant can help you define the problem and find the opportunity.

2.) Write down an objective description of your goal. If you have a sales objective in mind, like increasing revenue, the question is "by how much?"

3.) List expectations. Do you just want a quick answer, or do you want the consultant to participate over a period of time? Do you expect them to visit often or just talk to you over the phone? What kind of reports or analyses do you want?

4.) List prospective companies/consultants that might be able to meet your criteria. Consult industry directories, call managers at other stations within your group or within your network of other managers, check magazine ads and open your direct mail advertising from consultants.

5.) Before calling consultants, write down questions. For example: Are they available for your market? How do they like to work? What do they expect from you? What is the most important thing they want to know about you and your station? Have they had experience with a problem like the one you have described to them? How will they go about solving your problem? What kind of time frame would be reasonable to expect results? How do they know that?

6.) Contact them to determine their availability in your market. Determine their expertise and their cost structure, and listen carefully to how well you relate to them.

7.) Verify expertise with existing clients.

8.) Prepare a written contract.

A consultant should be in "partnership" with your goals, objectives, strategies and tactics. You do not have to agree on every decision, but the consultant's input should be valuable in helping you reach your decision.

A story is told about Charles Steinmetz, a retired electrical genius from General Electric. He consulted for his former company when it had a serious problem with some machinery. He walked around the equipment, made a few tests and placed a chalk mark where he believed the problem to be. The workers disassembled the machine and, sure enough, the problem was where Steinmetz said it was. Later, the company received a bill for $10,000. Company officials were shocked and demanded an itemized bill, which Steinmetz agreed to send. It read: Making one chalk mark: $1. Knowing where to put it: $9,999.

Chapter 12

No Excuses

Careful Communication

By Gina Gallagher

The true meaning of your communication is the response you get. One of the most challenging parts of the manager's job is to function as an "Unmanager." The reality is that the sales staff recognizes your authority limits and may try to manipulate the situation by not making your request a priority.

Your communication can be a major asset or a major liability. The following behavior change and communication models may assist you in establishing more effective communication. You will establish yourself as a credible leader, and gain better compliance from your staff.

- **One of management's major challenges is expressing dissatisfaction and obtaining not only change, but agreement that change is needed.**
- **A problem description statement should describe a recurring behavior in a way that leaves no opening for counterattack or excuses.**
- **The statement should describe an effect of the behavior on others.**
- **Follow up an employee's complaint or observation with precise questioning that focuses on solutions.**

Behavior Change Model

• One of management's major problems is expressing dissatisfaction and obtaining change.

• The outcome we look for is not only change but also agreement for change.

• We must set criteria to measure whether change occurs and whether it is satisfactory.

Problem Description Statement

• The statement describes a recurring behavior in a way which indicates appropriate responses and leaves no room for counterattack or excuses.

- The statement has four parts: A factual report of the behavior; a factual report on the results of that behavior; a report on the effect of that behavior on the manager or group; agreement for compliance.
- The problem description statement is worded in a way that leaves no opening for excuses or questioning the value of the behavior.
- Problem description statements treat excuses and reasons as irrelevant and return to the original statement whenever stock responses are received.
- You are not expressing an opinion.
- Once acceptance of the statement is obtained, then problem-solving and action toward behavior change can take place.

Case Study 1:

Situation: Employee turns in reports late for the third time within six months.

Manager: When you give me reports later than the set deadline, I don't have time to prepare my report for the president and I don't feel confident that I can explain what has happened satisfactorily.

Or:

Manager: When you don't get reports to me on time without giving me the warning we agreed on, I don't have time to change my managers' meeting. When this occurs, I am unable to keep the agreements I have with them to supply accurate information.

Review:

- First part of the problem description statement names a behavior which can or cannot be agreed to. That is, was there a specific deadline? Did the employee give adequate warning? These questions refer to elements which were previously made explicit and are readily verifiable and can be agreed to.
- The second part of the statement is an external result which can be understood by the other person and is totally within your experience. It can contain factual details or the effect on others. This part also assumes the employee is committed to producing the results intended by the manager.
- The final part puts you into the statement. The results have an impact on you and, being in a working relationship with you, the employee cares about those results. This part will always be an expression about you, never disguised comments about the other person.

Communications Model

• In most situations, the manager is in the position of knowing less about the specific situation than the employee.

• In most cases, you will want to gather more information before getting very far into solving problems or making suggestions.

• When you ask a perception model question, you get high-frequency answers.

• The first step in questioning is to set a frame or context for the employee. Otherwise, employees may feel confused and wonder where the conversation is going or what the manager is after.

• "Tell me about it" also leaves the employee not knowing what information to give or how to give it. Framing can be used to overcome these problems.

Case Study 2:

Statement: This program doesn't work.

Framing: You've mentioned the problems of this program getting off the ground. I heard this before, and I really don't have the full information. To be able to decide how to proceed, there are a few things I need to know about what's been happening. I'll have to ask you a few questions so we can decide how to solve this with some shared information.

Question Model

Through precise questioning and follow-up to an employee's complaint, the manager can get the employee to focus on solutions. Here are some examples.

Noun Blockbuster: A noun might be naming more than one thing or referring to something unknown in some way.

Question: Which one, specifically? Which part of the program, specifically?

Question the Verb: How, specifically, is it working or not working?

Universal Blockbuster: A pronoun or adjective suggesting that a whole group or class is the same or is included in the situation. Common words are: all, everyone, none, only.

Statement: None of these systems works.

Question: Are there any exceptions?

Comparable Blockbuster: An adjective comparing one item or group to another without stating what it is compared to.

Question: Adjective compared to what?

Boundary Crossing: Whenever a word or phrase indicates that something is impossible or necessary. Common words: can't, must, have to, no way.

Statement: There is no way we can sell these programs.

Question: What stops us from doing it? What will happen if we do?

Case Study 3:

Employee: We can't reach the manufacturer.

Manager: What stops you from reaching them? Who is "we"?

Employee: It takes too much time.

Manager: What, specifically, takes too much time?

Employee: We have to look up all of the information and call four or five times.

Manager: Are there any times when you can reach the manufacturer?

Employee: Yes.

Manager: What else can you do to reach the manufacturer?

The linguistic patterns used in all cases above direct and narrow the dialogue to achieve the intended outcome. We all speak and interact using a variety of deletions and distortion. The effective communicator, however, can direct the interaction by narrowing in on the specifics.

Chapter 13

Obstacles To Perfection

By Dave Gifford

In Chapter Two, I gave a complete job description for the position of sales manager. Maybe for the perfect sales manager? The problem is that no one is perfect. In fact, I have never met anybody in this business who is "overqualified" for whatever they're doing.

So what are these day-to-day realities that prohibit sales managers from being letter-perfect?

- **Managing the salespeople and the sales effort is only part of a sales manager's job.**
- **Either you manage the sales effort or the sales effort manages you.**
- **Either you manage the salespeople or the salespeople manage you.**
- **Unless you get some training on your own, you're probably not going to get any real management training in this business.**

It Comes With The Territory

1.) Not included in any job description, however complete, is the fact that you have to manage people not just as salespeople but as human beings. You also have to manage your boss, sometimes the owner, criticism, pressure, stress, your patience, disappointment, discouragement, anger, company policies, jealousies, frustrations, "things," interruptions, the telephone, money, your personal life, your significant other, your ambitions, time, your personal guilt, a crisis, another crisis, etc. But it comes with the territory, doesn't it?

2.) There is no loyalty to a company.

3.) Eventually, for one reason or another, everyone will leave your station — including you.

4.) For most survivors, a career in Radio is made up, over time, from a series of "temporary" jobs.

5.) Unless you divide your salespeople into teams or pay them significantly for their production as a team, there is no such thing as teamwork on a sales staff; it's every man and woman for themselves. Rather than trying to build a team, you're better off hiring the right people in the first place.

6.) Except for those on your staff who are totally committed to Radio as a career, everyone else has a hidden agenda. Maybe someone on your staff wants your job, or is interviewing for a sales management position elsewhere, or wants to sell for another station with higher ratings, or just doesn't want to work for you anymore, or wants to go into TV sales or get out of the broadcasting business altogether, or wants their own business (like an ad agency), or wants to make a career move just to change their life, or wants to go back to college, or wants to get married, or wants to get a divorce, or has every intention of staying but no intention of working any harder (or smarter) to make any more money, etc.

No Instant Wisdom

7.) On the day you were first appointed sales manager, you were not suddenly imbued with "wisdom."

8.) Unless you get some on your own, you're probably not going to get any real management training in this business. Not if it's going to cost money, that is. Ridiculous!

9.) Management time is overtime.

10.) For the sales manager, life's report card is your station's total billing vs. this month's billing target.

11.) "Friday's problem" (following a poor sales week) is your problem.

12.) Advertiser demand, created in part from the pressures that more new accounts put on your inventory, is a function of how good you are as a sales manager.

Manage Or Be Managed

13.) Either you manage the sales effort or the sales effort manages you.

14.) Either you manage the salespeople or the salespeople manage you.

15.) The most certain thing about this business is the certainty of change. Better make friends with your future.

16.) There are two kinds of stress for sales managers: Positive stress from achieving your billing goals through hard work, and negative stress from not achieving your billing goals, no matter how hard you work. And, since it's within every sales manager's power to determine which stress they're going to live with, the difference comes down to working smarter, not harder.

17.) Sales managers have one objective and one objective only: To advance their careers by exceeding the station's revenue goals.

18.) As sales manager, you're only as good as your sales staff.

19.) Your invitation to anarchy comes when you fail to manage what must be managed.

20.) "There is no try. There is only do or do not." — Yoda

Chapter 14

Share Cost For Profit

By Dwight Case

I have been working on a project on the central coast of California for a while and have had a good opportunity to visit with many of the managers of the "too many" Radio stations.

To give you a feel for the area, it is about 90 miles long, 15 miles wide and encompasses three towns of reasonable size about 30 miles apart. Chain stores abound, there is a university … and … 32 (thirty-two!) Radio stations.

Some LMAs and Duopolies are in play. But my thought is that we might put some creativity to work here to get at some profit-producing revenue.

The Consolidation Concept

Let's call a town hall meeting for GMs, with the following agenda: 1. Should there be one GM for all 32 stations? 2. Should there be one sales manager, program director, engineer, bookkeeper, etc.? 3. Should the 10 best salespeople sell all the stations — or represent all the stations with 200 of the key clients in the area? 4. Can we invent a software program where all stations can be trafficked, invoiced, statemented at one location … one person …? 5. Should all stations simulcast from 10 p.m. to 5 a.m.? 6. Can there be one telemarketing company setting appointments for all stations from just one location? 7. Can we have one office building for all stations? 8. Can we have one production unit per language to produce speculative commercials and sold commercials?

Some of this thinking is being done by such companies as shopping centers, etc. The concept is to consolidate costs and enhance services so you can entice a buyer to your product and fulfill the need for advertising.

Estimating Costs Vs. Profits

As a thought-starter, let's give out 3-by-5 cards with the following information: If we have 32 stations, then it is possible to have: 32 GMs; 32 SMs; 32 PDs; 32 Bookkeepers; 32 Engineers; 32 Morning People; 128 Announcers; 24 Part-timers; 128 Salespeople; 32 Leases; 32 Insurance Payments.

Multiply that total by $10 per hour on average and, well, you know where I'm going. Here's my question: If you don't do this, what is your alternative?

Chapter 15

Some Antics With Semantics

Managing Vs. Leading

By Chris Gable

- **Managing may equal mediocrity. Leading takes a different course.**
- **Leading involves vision, doing, making things happen.**
- **Your choice of job titles says a lot about how you approach your tasks, mission and goals.**
- **Examine your setup. Remember, you are not destined to repeat the errors of the past unless you choose to do so.**

Manage or lead. For many, there are only subtle differences between the two, but I believe the difference is as wide as that between those who succeed and those who excel. More to the point, it is a fundamental difference of attitude, style and ultimate goal.

A quick look at the dictionary shows that one who leads is typically one who guides by going first, serves as a channel for or directs the operation. Manage, by definition, conjures up some rather scary prospects, such as to make and keep submissive, to alter by manipulation and to get by.

More Leaders, Fewer Managers

The basic difference comes down to dealing with what is (managing) or dealing with what can be (leading). Ten or 20 years ago, a broadcast property could be properly managed and do very well. That's why Wall Street saw such possibility in our world. What they missed is that managing does not always win, and in today's economy it doesn't even guarantee success. Today, managing might even be compared to mediocrity, and we all know what that does to a broadcast property. It's an easy progression to the understanding that in our highly competitive and volatile business, the leaders will always win and the managers will fail.

Check most universities and institutions of higher learning and you'll certainly find many programs devoted to management, but few, if any, that deal with leadership. Interesting that you can get a degree in management, but the learning process for leadership is so fundamentally different that there is no degree program; yet, what we need so desperately are more leaders and fewer managers.

What's In A Title?

Think about the various titles we seek for ourselves or bestow on others. What do these titles say about ourselves and the way we accept responsibility and challenge? Finally, what do these titles say about the way we lead or manage, succeed or excel?

Enough serious reflection ... let's have some fun with ourselves and our titles.

- CEO, CFO, COO — Alphabet soup for corporate types. How is it that the folks who graduate from B-School end up with C in their title? Also, note that corporate-level positions get titles with three letters, while station-level positions usually are two-lettered, i.e., GM, AE, PD, MD, SM.
- Chairman — One of the few titles that really means what it says. The bigger and higher the chair, the greater the power of the chairman. The transition from lettered title to a two-syllable name makes for a powerful distinction.
- Vice President — Get to handle the good stuff, all the while knowing that they're on the way to being president someday (even if they have to buy their own).
- Sales Representative — I always liked this because it says up-front that I sell and that I represent something or someone. In fact, I represent my station to the client, and I also represent the client to my station and its audience. You can keep the account exec./sales consultant stuff. I never managed accounts; that's for bookkeepers. And I know few people who hold consultants in high regard. Let's face it, a consultant is usually someone you bring in to solve problems you can't or won't deal with. It's tough to admit that kind of vulnerability to anyone. So I'll keep the representative role. It keeps me honest, open and always responsible to both sides of the equation.
- Program Director (and the various manager-titled positions often associated with it) — Whose program, and what is directed? In the motion picture industry, the big names are producers and executive producers, while the directors are artists and impressionists. Given the state of most Radio station affairs, perhaps the title executive producer would be more appropriate.
- Listeners/audience/demos — In the Reis and Trout world of

thinking, we may be advertising our expectations or lack thereof by our definition of the people we target with our product. Do they really listen? And is listening enough? An audience is captive, potentially more involved and is usually in that mode by choice. Demos just are too impersonal for consideration. No one really is a typical anything and would be insulted if you said so.

Remember, as broadcaster Rush Limbaugh often says: "Words do have meaning." Instead of blindly naming names and charting positions, attach meaning to your words, titles, jobs and tasks, and reflect that meaning with words, thoughts and deeds.

Normal job titles prescribed by an industry are fine for convention, normality and consistency. Fortunately, broadcasting requires a much different approach when success is the goal. Go ahead and change the title on your business card. It's the first step in a long line of changes you'll soon make as a leader.

Chapter 16

Down Your Throat Marketing

And In Your Ears

By Bill Burton

"Down your throat" marketing comes from Phil Guarascio, general manager for General Motors' North American operations, marketing and advertising. I've adopted it.

Guarascio could well be the top marketing director in the United States today — and certainly the highest-profile. He is part of the new thinking at General Motors. It's my belief that the further he goes, the further General Motors will go.

Whatever It Takes

Down Your Throat marketing is whatever it takes to sell consumers. While General Motors has new, quality products like Saturn, Cadillac STS and the Geo Prizm, the manufacturer's challenge is to recapture America and the world. So, old thinking, like the old General Motors, is in the back seat.

The same is true for Radio as a medium. Target marketing will continue to accelerate with the need to get closer to the potential consumer through niche marketing. All of which plays into today's Radio.

I asked Lou Schultz, executive vice president and media director for Lintas: Campbell-Ewald, what he would do if he were an automobile dealer.

"It wouldn't be traditional advertising. I would use whatever it takes to get consumers into the showroom. I'd have parties. I'd use an untraditional medium." With that I responded: "That's the new Radio, Lou. That is ideal to drive potential buyers into the showroom." He said: "Exactly." The new Radio is a down-your-throat, in-your-ears sales vehicle designed for today's lifestyle, hitting right in the middle of the target.

An example of how GM is using this approach is Chevrolet's S-10 pickup campaign, called Tune-It-Up. It's a Radio rebate campaign (which supposedly can't be done because of the disclaimer problem, but Chevrolet is doing it). It works like this: If you buy an S-10 now, you get $750 in cash or you can take $500 plus a choice of electronics gifts.

Reinventing Radio

Our Detroit Radio Advertising Group feels so strongly about the new Radio medium that we designed a new Radio presentation. We set the stage with decision-makers by stating the following: When something's been around for a long time and has served you well, many times it gets taken for granted — we think that's happened with one of the most dynamic medium of all, Radio.

Then we have them close their eyes and visualize there's no more Radio. And, from that, we reinvent Radio and make it a whole new exciting medium under the title "Get Me Radio."

Get Me Radio turned on the marketplace. That's the battle cry we're hearing from more and more informed marketeers who want to make something happen. Radio is the perfect weapon for target and niche marketing.

One presentation is primarily designed for decision-makers: "Don't Take No From A Person Who Can't Say Yes," to bring them up to date on the dynamics of Radio in the '90s. It focuses on Radio's great ability to deliver mobility, targetability and that all-important sales ingredient, frequency.

With the fractionalization of television, cable and so many other media, Radio is being rediscovered ... perhaps even reinvented by marketeers on the cutting edge.

See What You Sell

Some people look through the small end of a telescope; others look through the large end, so they see the same thing in totally different perspectives. Are you seeing and selling the Radio of yesterday, or are you focusing on the big picture and the dynamics of Radio today? Let me strongly suggest that all of you great sellers sell the dynamics of the new Radio. We've got the best product with the best salespeople. Radio's future is now.

Chapter 17

How To Welcome New Employees

By Jack M. Rattigan

The same challenges face almost everybody in broadcasting: Where can I find good people? Once I find them, how can I train them? How can I make and keep them productive? How can I build loyalty? How can I keep the competition from stealing away the really good ones?

While there are no guarantees, the following are successful approaches you should use to welcome new employees and ensure that the best ones stay around for a while.

- **Day One: Remember what it was like to be the new kid on the job? What did you wish had been different?**
- **The general manager should play host the first day, walk the employee around the station and introduce them to each staff member.**
- **Make sure each staff member explains their part in the station's operations.**
- **Assign a "big brother/big sister," someone to whom the new employee can comfortably direct questions.**
- **The First Week: Have a written agenda for the employee to spend time in each department.**

continued

Golden Rules

The New Employee: Above all, you must never forget that you were once the new kid on the job. Try to remember how you felt. What were your thoughts, questions, worries? What did you wish you had been told? What did you wish had been different? Was there a job or boss that made your first days easy? If so, review the situation and recreate it. In other words, put yourself in the place of the new employee. You have heard it before: Treat others as you would like others to treat you.

The First Day: First impressions are lasting. If you're the general manager, play host. Explain all company policies and procedures as well as the chain of command. Give the new employee a policy manual. (Your station should have one.) Show them around the workplace and introduce them to everyone on staff. Have each person explain their part of the station's operation. In an informal atmosphere, have the new employee ask questions freely about each staff member and their duties. Let them know that you don't expect them to remember everyone and understand everything the first day. Assign them a "big brother/big sister," someone to whom they can direct questions — questions they may not want to ask a supervisor or general manager.

Have An Agenda

The Remaining Days Of The First Week: Have an agenda for the new employee. Have them spend time in each department — sitting in to observe on-air activity, watching the production of a commercial or station promo, spending a half day in traffic, accounting and the business office. Have them attend a promotion and sales meeting and take part in the first available "talent appearance," remote or station-sponsored activity. Have them spend time with the chief engineer and, yes, go to the transmitter site. By now, many of you are saying: "We don't have time for all that." You should make time. It is an investment in what can be a long and productive association with this new team player.

Open The Lines Of Communication

On The 10th Day: Meet informally with the employee. Ask lots of questions. Do they understand the job? Encourage them to ask questions. Be supportive.

On The 13th Day: Conduct an informal but detailed interview: How is it going? What do they like most about the job and the station? What do they like least? Do they have any ideas on how their job could be more productive?

During The Second, Third and Fourth Weeks: Continue informal meetings or just stop by their work area. Continue to encourage two-way communication. Remind them of the "big brother/big sister" system. Ask how it is working. Continue to be supportive.

If you find the new employee will not make any suggestions and does not feel comfortable, you have not done your job in the first 30 days.

Ongoing Encouragement: Frequent informal exchanges should continue forever. A team player has to be nourished every day from the start. Let new employees and all your staff know that you enjoy working with them and appreciate their contribution to the station. Follow the Minute Manager Rule: Manage by walking around. In fact, re-read *Leadership and the One-Minute Manager* once every six months, and certainly the weekend before a new employee comes on board. It will help you help the new employee become a productive, loyal, long-term team player.

continued

- **The Second, Third And Fourth Weeks: Meet informally with the new employee. Encourage two-way communication. Be supportive.**
- **Give ongoing encouragement. Let all your employees know how much you appreciate their work.**

Chapter 18

Myth Management

By Rick Ott

Quite often, a lame notion becomes widely accepted as truthful wisdom simply because it's repeated over and over. It's about time we looked at two of the biggest Radio myths that keep getting repeated, and acknowledge that things really don't happen that way.

- **The thinner your demos, the more difficult they are to sell. The name of the game is, always has been and always will be: The more listeners you have, the more money you make.**
- **Giving a sales staff another station to sell — as can happen with an LMA or duopoly situation — only adds to its problems.**
- **Having one sales staff represent two stations will probably result in less revenue than the stations are capable of earning.**

Too Thin To Win

Myth: Niche programming is the wave of the future. Radio stations are becoming evermore specialized in their programming and marketing, targeting thinner-than-ever demo slices. Broadcasting is becoming "narrowcasting," and stations that want to survive and thrive must "superserve" their thinly defined niche or core.

Truth: It just doesn't happen that way. Sure, Radio is more fragmented than ever. That's because there are more stations on the air than ever. Everyone's got a thinner slice of the audience pie, but that doesn't mean more stations are programming to thinner demo slices.

A dozen different, highly specialized formats that appeal to niches could be created. Want to target male teens? Preteens? Female college students? Black males 34-39? Hispanic females 41-47? People with net worths over $1 million? Retirees 68-plus? The blueprints presently exist for formats that can appeal to any thin demo slice you want.

But who wants them? The thinner your demos, the more difficult they are to sell. Targeting some niche means starvation. The name of the game in Radio is, always has been and always will be: The more people who listen to your station, the more money you make.

So what we really have are more stations targeting the same fairly wide demos (25-54) with the same old formats. Every once in a while, a station adopts a true niche format, only to end up adjusting it wider or giving up on it entirely. Even public Radio is targeting fairly wide. Although they don't depend on ad revenue to survive, they still want as many listeners 25-plus as they can get.

Another Station, Another Burden

Myth: A sales staff that represents two stations will have greater advantage over, and bring in more revenue than, a staff that represents only one station. When you pare two sales forces down to one, and give the remaining force two stations to sell — as can happen with an LMA or duopoly situation — you'll bring in more revenue at half the cost. And the competition will be left behind.

Truth: It just doesn't happen that way. Adding another station to a sales staff's plate only adds to its problems. Another station, another burden. Isn't selling one station hard enough?

Tried selling them in combo, have you? If so, you've discovered there's no advantage there. Why? Because most buyers don't want the combo. That's true even if both stations have great ratings.

Yes, selling two stations with one sales staff can reduce your expenses. But it won't bring in more revenue. In fact, it will probably bring in significantly less revenue than your stations are capable of earning. The top-billing stations in most every market have a sales staff that concentrates on that station only. In fact, some stations now have two sales staffs, one to handle agencies and the other to handle directs. One station, two sales staffs. Opposite of the myth, because the myth isn't really the way things work.

Chapter 19

Swinging Signals

Understanding AM And FM Signals

By William P. Suffa

- **The FCC coverage contour levels are based on 1950s assumptions.**
- **The signal strength chosen for the coverage map will affect the size of the contour.**
- **All coverage predictions are based on statistical methods. Your mileage will vary.**

If you can't hear it, you can't sell it. That assumption often provokes one of the two questions most frequently asked of a broadcast consulting engineer: "How far will my station cover?" or "Why is our signal area nothing like the coverage map I have?" The response usually leads to some of the most frustrating discussions among owners, managers and the station's consultant.

The question of coverage is difficult to answer by even the best engineer. Many factors affect the Radio signal as it travels from transmitter to receiver. Some of these factors — power, antenna type, antenna height, AM ground system and transmitter location — are within the station's control (and FCC limits, of course). Other factors — atmospheric conditions, weather, foliage and interference — are most often beyond the control of either the station or engineer. In fact, these uncontrollable factors make any coverage prediction ambiguous and frustrating.

So what is "coverage," anyway? And why does the sales map of that little class A station in the suburbs look better than that of my big class B station?

The problem in defining coverage is this: Radio signals decrease in strength as they move away from the transmitter, but they never go away completely. Instead, they weaken to the point where receivers can no longer detect the signal. And that point varies from receiver to receiver.

Engineers, being fascinated by numbers, use statistics to compute and define coverage. And, as any good accountant can tell you, manipulating numbers the right way can produce almost any result you want. For that reason, it is important to understand how the on-paper coverage of your station is computed, and what real-life factors influence the actual reception of your signal. And since AM and FM are much different, only FM coverage will be dealt with here.

Signal Schemes Date Back To '50s

In the early days of FM, the FCC undertook tests to determine the signal strength necessary to provide usable, interference-free coverage to the average monophonic Radio receiver, with an antenna 30 feet above ground. Signal strengths were chosen for each class of station (then A, B or C) to provide reliable coverage that matched the earliest licensing scheme, basing classes on geographical areas, such as (A) local communities, (B) suburban areas and (C) rural areas. Ultimately, a 1.0 mV/m signal was considered "usable" for class A and C stations, and 0.5 mV/m was considered "usable" for class B stations. These signal levels form the basis of the FCC protections against interference between stations.

So, an assumption about the performance of an "average" Radio receiver of the 1950s is used to define the signal strength at which reliable coverage is achieved, although today most FM stations are in stereo and more susceptible to interference. As recently as 1984, the FCC affirmed that stereo service is a signal "enhancement" and should not be considered in predicting service or interference (hello, is anyone home?).

Of course, it is recognized that Radio signals can travel far beyond the "protected" contours, particularly in areas with favorable terrain and low interference levels. Engineers may sometimes be asked to select a somewhat lower usable signal level when preparing sales maps, thus showing better coverage than on FCC maps, which are based on the 1 mV/m standard. This sometimes leads to confusion when comparing different stations' maps which are not based on the same signal levels.

Prediction Methods

A more difficult dilemma occurs when discussing prediction methods. The prediction methods and assumptions used can influence the coverage shown on your map. The FCC specifies use of one general method for all its filings but allows other methods in certain circumstances. A terrain-sensitive calculation, such as the Longley-Rice or Tech Note 101 method, can be employed with reasonable accuracy.

Compare Apples To Apples

In preparing coverage or sales maps, discuss carefully with your engineer the appropriate signal level to ensure that the maps accurately reflect the coverage. A 1 mV/m might be adequate in suburban areas, but 0.5 mV/m might suffice in the flat, rural areas. In comparing the coverage of two stations, particularly when a station purchase is involved, be sure to compare apples to apples. If the coverage seems too good to be true, it may very well be. After all, if I could make every station cover half the known planet, I'd be sitting on a desert island right about now.

Chapter 20

Success Or Failure?

The Leading Indicators

By Rick Ott

As you may have noticed, the Radio industry has not escaped the effects of the Peter Principle (people tend to rise to their level of incompetence). As in every other industry, there are broadcast industry managers — from owners and corporate executives, to general managers, sales managers and program directors — who consistently demonstrate remarkable incompetence.

- **People you'd never expect to be good managers grow in competence, and vice versa.**
- **Leading indicators of eventual failure as a manager include demonstrations of power, reluctance to delegate and becoming territorial and/or defensive.**
- **The three leading indicators of eventual success as a manager include empowering subordinates, supporting peers and seeing the bigger picture.**

The funny thing about management is that you never know who will work out as a manager, and will fail, until he or she actually becomes a manager. Quite often, people who you'd never expect to be good at it grow in competence, while people who look like sure bets fail miserably.

Although it's almost impossible to determine a person's chances for success before he or she is promoted into management, I've identified a few leading indicators — traits that newly appointed managers tend to exhibit, that point to eventual success or failure. These leading indicators usually become evident in the first 90 days of a person's appointment to a managerial position.

The Failure Indicators

Here are three leading indicators of eventual failure as a manager:

1.) *Demonstrations of power.* The failure-destined manager is constantly reminding others "who's in charge." This may include casual comments that berate others, or suggestions that few others "know what they're doing." This manager undermines subordinates by criticizing and changing their decisions, and engaging in full-blown power plays against peers, trying to maneuver themselves into positions of authority over as many others as possible. And, they never admit mistakes, as they believe that doing so would puncture their powerful ego, or raise questions about their competence.

2.) *Reluctance to delegate.* When a new manager refuses to let go of his or her former duties, or insists on "keeping his hands in things," by staring over the shoulder of his or her replacement, trouble is ahead. These managers may refuse to empower their people with any meaningful decision-making authority, insisting that virtually everything be "run by them" for approval.

3.) *Territorial and/or defensive.* Because they view many others (especially peers inside and outside the company) as threats to their position or authority, these managers become very defensive and territorial. They try to keep other competent people away, or may refuse to cooperate with others in the picture who are more competent. They will undermine, or even sabotage the work of peers, since they feel the success of others takes away from their own success.

(*Note:* The primary underlying cause of the above three indicators is a lack of self-confidence. Some people are ambitious and power-hungry on one hand, but lack a belief in their own ability to handle this power, on the other hand.)

The Success Indicators

Here are three leading indicators of eventual success as a manager:

1.) *Empowers subordinates.* When a new manager understands that 80 percent of the job is bringing out the best in his or her subordinates, this manager is destined for success. He or she gives subordinates the authority to make decisions (within clearly defined parameters), and then supports their decisions. These managers recognize the special abilities and talents of their people, and encourage and cheerlead them in order to make the most of their attributes. They will try to make their people look good, often taking responsibility or admitting their own mistakes, rather than shifting the blame downward, thus lowering morale.

2.) *Supports peers.* These managers understand that their own success is largely tied to the success of their peers, and the station/company as a whole. They are true team players, cooperating, supporting and encouraging other managers.

3.) *Sees the bigger picture.* As a manager, he or she can now step back and see the entire picture, not just the detailed workings of his or her department. These managers develop an understanding and appreciation of the entire station or company, and the ways in which all the departments or divisions work together as a complete team. They make decisions based on both the detailed and big picture, considering the wide-ranging ramifications of their decisions.

Chapter 21

Laughing Matters

Using Humor In Business

By Dr. Sharon Crain

When a survey of 200 male executives summarized their top 10 reasons women wouldn't make it to the top in their profession, reason No. 3 was because women don't have a sense of humor.

- **Be appropriate. Use humor relevant to the situation.**
- **Practice delivery skills.**
- **Be prepared. "Prepared" witty quips tend to become spontaneous.**
- **Be a thief. Be forever on the alert for clever ways to make a point.**

My first impression was that it must have been a misprint. Then I began to focus on a form of behavior among many professional males, which I term bantering. They tease and "roast" each other incessantly. Women are rarely included — and then often as the "roastee."

I began to realize that women generally don't engage in this form of jocularity. We often express our humor by relating past funny incidents about other people. By contrast, where male humor tends to be interactive, present-oriented and directed toward a group member, women's humor tends to be reactive, past-oriented and directed toward non-group members.

These differences make sense if we think back to our teens. While adolescent boys were engaging in "king-of-the-mountain" hierarchical games, complete with insults and barbs, girls were intent on fostering agreement. The girl who attempted to rise above the rest of the group was quickly brought back to an equal level.

Our culture has trained us to handle interpersonal relationships in a more serious manner. And how men can walk into a meeting kidding each other, tear each other apart during the meeting and walk out arm-in-arm has long been a mystery to many women.

Humor Sells

Research indicates that humor is a big factor in ensuring professional success. In one study, the director of development of a major university gave 100 speeches to alumni groups and requested funds for the university. The speeches were identical, with one exception. In 50, he told a short, humorous anecdote about the university, and in the other 50 he did not. As a result, he raised more than 50 percent more from the groups where he used humor.

Making others laugh is a primary way to build rapport in professional life. This ability to build empathy and harmony between people is the basis for influencing others, whether it means drawing more listeners to your station, selling more advertising or being a more effective manager.

Humor Reduces Stress

A Duke University study conducted more than 50 years ago concluded that the only functional purpose of laughter is to reduce stress. Next time you find yourself in a negotiation deadlock or a disagreement with staff at your station, notice what happens when suddenly someone delivers the magical funny remark. Note how the tone of the group immediately changes and who becomes the hero of the moment.

Or, when your plan or idea has just been rejected by the group, notice how doubling your intensity is seldom successful. Next time, prepare a humorous remark in the event of rejection, deliver it at the magic moment and notice the difference. As in the negotiation situation, appropriate humor reduces the level of conflict and shifts the group toward a more positive mind-set. This new, positive tone sets the stage for you to win more of what you want from colleagues as well as superiors.

Humor Is A Skill

Even though you may not think of yourself as a source of laughter, you can quickly develop this skill. Here are some guidelines:

1.) *Be Appropriate.* To reduce the risk of bombing: a) Do not announce that you intend to be funny. b) Use humor relevant to the situation. c) Follow rules a & b and, if no one laughs, keep going — they will never know.

2.) *Practice Delivery Skills.* Humor by its very nature is based on a degree of irreverence. Therefore, it should be delivered with confidence. Simple delivery guidelines include: a) Cut out all nonessential words. b) Use concrete, simple words (i.e., weird, not psychotic). c) Learn which words to emphasize. d) Practice learning to pause — the basis of timing.

3.) *Be Prepared.* As queen of the great-response-three-hours-too-late, I finally wised up and prepared myself with more memorable comments than my flat-footed past would suggest. These "prepared" quips have now become spontaneous.

4.) *Be A Thief.* Be forever on the alert for clever ways to make a point. "Lead with your teeth" is the way a witty corporate president reminded his staff to smile at customers.

My favorite piece of pilfered humor comes from a woman judge in Phoenix. One of the male staff in her courtroom made the error of calling her "Hon." She responded with: "Please call me by my appropriate name — Attila!"

Chapter 22

Tie Advertising Efforts To The Bottom Line

Show An Advertiser That Their Advertising Works

By Dr. Philip J. LeNoble

How many times have you heard a prospective client say: "Newspaper is my best source of advertising"? How do they know?

This is one of the most difficult tasks an advertiser or Radio executive faces. How do you prove an ad campaign works? Actually, several methods exist of tying clients' advertising efforts to their own bottom line.

One sure way is to have clients ask their customers a specific question, such as: "Did you hear our commercial on Station X?" This gives the respondent a yes or no option. You can help the recall effort by offering to place a sign on the door or window leading into the store stating: "As advertised on Station X." Place a similar placard in the store next to the item being advertised on your station.

- **Combine consumer inquiries with in-store signage to determine Radio's effectiveness in drumming up business for your client.**
- **A higher frequency of advertising yields more sales. The more exposure to an ad, the more a consumer will use a product.**
- **By determining your client's market share before and after a schedule, you can show how your station made a difference in their overall growth.**
- **The Return On Investment formula can also demonstrate Radio advertising's effectiveness for prospective clients.**

Take A Number

Research has found that this combination of direct questioning and in-store signage can help the client measure the station's effectiveness. When the customer confirms that they heard the ad on Station X, a sticker bearing the station's logo might be attached to the sales invoice. At the end of the week, the stickers can be counted and the results of the station's delivery can be counted in sales.

While these are simple ways to help quantify Radio's persuasiveness, there are other means to measure a good, sustained campaign. One way is to divide your client's total gross sales by the total gross sales of that industry in your market to determine their market share. (The Census of Retail Trade, published every five years, contains that information by market.) Taken before an annual or semiannual schedule and again following the schedule, market share might reveal how your station made a distinguishable difference in your client's overall market growth and could lead to a renewal.

Frequent Buyer Bonus

As the late retail icon Sam Walton noted: "Funny thing happens when you stop inviting folks to come to your store." A study in 1986 by the Advertising Research Foundation and the Association of Business Publishers showed that higher frequency of advertising yields up to 600 percent more sales in less than a year, compared to the minimal gains attained by only modest increases in advertising (200 percent and lower). W.R. Simmons & Associates Research found that people who had been exposed to multiple ads used the product "significantly more" than those who had been exposed to the ad only once.

Positive feelings toward a brand or store are directly related to advertising exposure. A 1990 report by the American Association of Advertising Agencies demonstrated that during the Great Depression, market leaders of 1925 like Coca-Cola, Kodak, Kellogg, Campbell's, Lipton and Wrigley who maintained advertising throughout the era, sustained a market leadership that has yet to diminish.

A 1962 study conducted by Politz found that two closely spaced exposures to a given ad will boost a product's Brand Quality Rating an average of 35 points.

Multiply, Divide ... And Sell

Research conducted by Executive Decision Systems Inc. found still another measure of advertising effectiveness: the Return On Investment formula.

To use it, multiply the client's average sale by the gross profit (sales minus cost of inventory), then multiply that figure by the selling or closing rate. The result is the potential value of each prospect who enters the business establishment.

The potential value number is then divided into the monthly advertising schedule, which yields the number of prospects needed to pay for the schedule. Multiply this figure by the closing rate to find the number of sales needed to pay for the ad schedule, a break-even point expressed as gross sales.

The low number of sales needed to break even shows how little risk there is in advertising on your station. Try the formula, but only if the average sale is more than $70.

To further your understanding of advertising effectiveness, call the Association of National Advertisers (ANA) in New York and ask them about their text *Defining Advertising Goals for Measured Advertising Results and Marketplace Measurement.*

Make sales simple and help the advertiser know how to measure results. The bottom line is the renewal for another year.

Chapter 23

Making Equipment Sound Like New

By Roy Pressman

- **Consoles can be upgraded with new electronics for half the cost of new equipment.**
- **Simple maintenance steps can restore old cart machines to like-new condition.**
- **Replace the exciter to improve the sound and reliability of an older, functioning FM transmitter.**
- **Studio speakers can be repaired/refinished.**
- **Modulation monitors and audio processors can be shipped to the factory for modifications.**
- **Improve the sound of any microphone with a mike processor.**
- **Change studio acoustics by adding acoustic foam sound panels.**

In this climate of cutbacks and skeleton staffs, stations should be on the lookout for ways to be competitive without spending a fortune on new equipment.

A smart alternative is to update your present equipment. Many products today can give new life to old consoles, cart machines, audio processing, studio acoustics, monitoring equipment and transmitters.

Old Console, New Life

Your on-air console works fine, but it's old and tired. A comparable replacement would cost $5,000 to $12,000. But you can update your console with all-new electronics for around $2,000. It's just like putting a new engine in an old car.

Updates are not usually available from the manufacturer. Check with your equipment supplier for third-party manufacturers.

You can easily restore most cart machines to like-new condition by following these easy steps:

1.) Replace cart alignment tape (if over three years old).
2.) Replace record and playback heads every two years.
3.) Replace pinch rollers every six months.

4.) Clean heads daily.
5.) Demagnetize and align monthly.
6.) Replace old carts or rewind (yearly).

If you own ITC cart machines, there are several plug-in products from third-party manufacturers that will improve the overall sonic performance. ITC also has update kits available for Series 99 machines. Check with the manufacturer or your equipment supplier.

Transmitter Transformation

It doesn't take a rocket scientist to figure out the easiest way to improve the sound and reliability of an older, functioning FM transmitter: Just replace the exciter. This modification takes only a few minutes and costs $4,000 to $6,000. Check with the manufacturer of your transmitter for other possible updates. If your transmitter has serious problems, replace it with a new one. If you can't afford a new one, look into purchasing a used transmitter with a new exciter.

Studio speakers can be repaired. Defective elements can be removed or replaced, and grill cloths are easily fixed. Your local cabinet shop can refinish the cabinets or add a fresh coat of paint to make those speakers look brand new.

Older modulation monitors are often inaccurate. This can rob your station of loudness and make you vulnerable to an FCC citation. Ship your monitor back to the factory for recalibration. If you desire added accuracy, add one of the new digital modulation meters/analyzers to your monitor (Wizard, Mod-Minder).

Some audio processors, such as the Optimod 8000 and 8100, can be updated by the factory. Pricing depends on condition of the unit, and turnaround times can be more than three weeks. The manufacturer can tell you what modifications apply to your unit. Many third-party plug-in cards are available, so check with your equipment supplier.

Get The Most From Your Mike

You can improve the sound of any microphone with a mike processor. Mike processors typically contain a compressor, limiter and equalizer, which allow you to adjust the sound to your exact taste.

Change the acoustics of your studio by adding acoustic foam sound panels (such as Sonex). These panels mount easily and give immediate results. If you need to improve studio isolation from outside noise, try installing prefabricated soundproof windows or soundproof doors.

If your console lacks certain features (such as mix minus), a multitude of special boxes and interfaces exist that can turn an otherwise dysfunctional console into something completely functional. Interfaces typically cost less than $300.

Consumer electronics such as cassette decks and CD players are easily adapted to professional applications. All you need is an interface and rack-mount hardware (only if you plan to mount the equipment in a rack). Consumer machines can sound unbelievably good at a fraction of the cost of professional machines. However, consumer equipment is not designed for continual use, so you could experience more frequent failures than usual.

Weighing Your Options

Look closely at your capital budget, then decide which equipment should be replaced and which can be updated. Remember, updating equipment can save you money in the short term, but new equipment will give you long-term results.

Chapter 24

Boosting Local Sales

By Richard Chapin

A genuine concern of mine over the last 10 years has finally become a reality for Radio managers. Owners, general managers and sales managers finally realize that they need to spend a lot more time on local business.

The easy money that many stations were accustomed to is gone. The warehousing of barter spots by the networks has put such pressure on the national and regional sales picture that the local Radio station is feeling it now more than ever.

Shamefully, management hasn't been working as hard as it should on local sales. Many general managers spend too much time reading the trades; studying advertisements regarding consultants, new formats, new automation equipment; worrying about another station moving into the market and reading the monthly newsletters from consultants and Washington attorneys. Managers also spend too much time on EBS non-essential meetings and busywork. If they would spend more of their time working with their sales departments, the station would benefit greatly.

- **The "easy money" is gone, and the local Radio station is feeling the pressure now more than ever.**
- **While Radio has survived primarily because of local retail business, management hasn't been working as hard as it should on local sales.**
- **Managers need to spend less time on busywork and more time on the streets with salespeople.**
- **With more pressure on local retailers, Radio stations will need innovation to compete. Talk about your success stories.**

Get Out On The Street

The person at the top needs to get out on the street. Go with the salespeople and the sales manager to the local retailer. Learn exactly why they aren't buying time on your station. Most retailers, bank presidents, company managers, etc. would certainly be more impressed with a visit from the GM than with all the basic sound arguments the account executive could offer.

Too often, top managers think of sales visits as beneath them or only a minor part of their job — if they feel any responsibility at all. During the 37 years that I ran my company, our managers had two basic obligations: pushing me to increase their sales promotion and promotion expenditures, and spending a lot of their time making calls with salespeople.

Radio has survived primarily because of local retail business, and now that much of the national spot has diminished, large-market Radio stations realize that they need to replace the lost business by turning inward and going local.

Share Success Stories

With more stations and more salespeople on the street, there is more pressure on the local retailer. It takes innovation to compete, and smart broadcasters have turned their stations' attention to those areas where Radio is superior in entertainment and information.

Radio still has one helluva job to do on the local scene, and we all know that as soon as we land a great local account, the ad agencies move in. We have survived because we have been innovative in spite of the constant agency rejections. Radio is unlike any other medium; it goes in the ears, not the eyes, and we work hard for retention.

So general managers and sales managers need to talk about their successes. Talk about how many tires you've sold, how many shirts you've sold, how many people showed up. Tell local retailers how you can sell their product. Work on your success stories, and don't be afraid to display them. The only place that they are effective is with the retail advertiser on the local level.

Radio is a great medium. It works better than most of the others when you give it a chance to do what it does best. Radio can work even better for local retailers if you show them how to use it right — and call on them often.

Chapter 25

The Teamwork Era

By Jack M. Rattigan

- **No man or woman is an island.**
- **Lead by example.**
- **Give credit to others.**
- **Everyone is important.**
- **Delegation is a key in teamwork.**
- **The day of the hard-nosed boss is over.**

To quote one of the great philosophers of the 20th century, Yogi Berra: "The future ain't what it used to be." Gary Fries, president/CEO of the RAB, puts it this way: "We cannot survive unless we change." Ken Blanchard says: "None of us is as smart as all of us." I agree with all the above and would like to add this: "We can't do it alone anymore." (Maybe we never could.) Taken together, all of these and other bits of wisdom make for valuable management philosophy in the '90s.

"No man (or woman) is an island." No one can do it all, alone. There is and always has been someone helping, someone adding to the original idea or giving support. It is called teamwork. The baseball pitcher can't pitch a perfect game without the catcher catching all the strikes. The football quarterback can't throw a perfect pass without the linemen holding back the other team. The fighter pilot can't fly into battle without the flight crew maintaining the plane in perfect condition.

Roll Up Your Sleeves

Lead by example. In Radio today, teamwork is more important than ever. ("The future ain't what it used to be.") And it often has been said that teamwork starts at the top. No one can be expected to be a team player if the boss isn't a team player. That means rolling up your sleeves and getting your hands dirty. It means going to station-sponsored activities like concerts, charity benefits, remotes on a Saturday afternoon, etc.

It means helping load the van. It means having lunch with an advertiser to say: "Thank you for your business." It means spending an evening at the transmitter to help the engineer get the station back on the air. It means never expecting your staff to do anything you wouldn't do. Three ways to teach teamwork are by example, by example and by example.

Give credit to others. Gen. Norman Schwarzkopf constantly gave credit to his troops and allies. He never forgot that Desert Storm was a joint effort. A Radio station's manager is, in a sense, a general and must appreciate the troops. When the station's ratings are good, give the program and air staff public praise. When a sales goal is achieved, the sales staff deserves widespread appreciation. The entire staff should share in the glory, because they contributed to the success.

Delegation is a key to teamwork. Any manager who thinks no one can do anything as well as they can is not a team player. A manager cannot get involved in a lot of activities unless department heads and the staff can make decisions on their own. A real team knows what is good for the station and takes pride in its accomplishments.

The Importance Factor

Everyone is important. Without the engineer, you would have no signal on the air; without the program department, you would have no product; without the sales staff, you would have no revenue; without the traffic department, you would have no commercial schedule; without the business office, you would have no invoices or payroll. Never forget the person who answers the phone. To the general public, the voices on the air and on the phone are the Radio station. Everyone plays a part and should feel that they're an important member of the station family. It is management's responsibility to let everyone know that they are appreciated.

The day of the hard-nosed boss is over. The 1990s manager must understand that staff members are human beings who deserve to be rewarded when they surpass the routine. They need to be warned when their performance is below standard. The staff needs to understand that "we are in this together." Like those on a lifeboat, if the other end of the boat goes down, so do you. The old-style boss — screaming, ranting and raving in the hall — will not develop a winning team. All that will result is an unhappy, unmotivated, job-hunting mob.

Management must recognize the importance of everyone working together and set a positive pace of cooperation. Management must be committed to lead, and to lead by being a part of the team.

Chapter 26

Making Training More Fun

Five Ideas

By Kathryn Maguire

- **The Play Phone Game helps staff brainstorm the best ways to set up appointments.**
- **Vendor Scavenger Hunt is a fun way to collect items for sales training meetings.**
- **Match Game helps staff learn vendor terms and objections.**
- **Freeze Tag Vendor Presentation Practice turns a childhood game into an exercise for developing presentations.**
- **Speaker Of The Month brings in people from the business community to help staff learn the language and needs of manufacturers and retailers.**

The Play Phone Game

Purchase a pair of play phones from your local toy store or just unhook a few telephones in your sales office. Use them for effect and to make the meeting more fun.

Discuss with your group the basic steps in getting an appointment with a manufacturer. Using an easel pad, brainstorm the best opening statement to use on the phone. List some credibility statements to use on the call. List each of the most common objections that come up on the phone, and brainstorm possible answers.

Get two volunteers on your staff to be manufacturer and Radio account executive. Give them each a play phone and instruct the AE to get an appointment with the manufacturer using the information you have discussed. As a follow-up to the meeting, hand out typed sheets with opening statements, credibility statements and objections with answers for the sales staff to use as cheat sheets.

Vendor Scavenger Hunt

Divide the sales staff into teams of two to three people. Give the teams a list of vendor/sales-related things to find and bring to the next sales meeting. The team that brings in the most things from the list wins a prize, like restaurant trade or an award certificate.

Here is a starter list: freestanding inserts (coupons in the Sunday newspaper), photograph of an end aisle display, a feature ad, a circular, a shelftalker, a deal sheet (a manufacturer's case promotion one-sheet), a trade magazine like *Supermarket News* or *Women's Wear Daily*, a success letter from a manufacturer, a signed contract from a manufacturer (station contract, that is — authentic, of course) and a manufacturer's annual report. At the end of this contest, you will have a lot of things to use in future sales training meetings. This game also makes vendor sales more tangible for AEs.

Match Game

This game is designed for learning vendor terms and definitions, but it also works for vendor objections and answers. Choose which way you would like to use this training game first.

On a piece of poster paper, make three or four rows, and paste or tape blank station note cards on the poster paper. If this is not possible, use folded pieces of plain paper. You must have an even number of cards on the poster paper. In no particular order, write terms on the inside of half of the cards. Then write definitions on the inside of the other half of the cards.

Divide the staff into two teams. The first team can "open" two cards to match a term with its definition. If they fail, they must close the cards and give the other team a chance. Each team gets a point for every match, and they continue playing until they miss. The team with the most points at the end of the game wins a prize.

Freeze Tag Vendor Presentation Practice

This is similar to the freeze tag you played when you were a child, but you won't be running around.

Start the meeting with a discussion of an initial appointment with a manufacturer. Talk about how to represent yourself. List questions to ask. Review probable manufacturer objections. Discuss the importance of getting the second appointment.

Ask two volunteers to be manufacturer and account executive. Strategically, the volunteers should be the least experienced at your station. You will find that the senior account executives will more heavily participate that way. Identifying each person's role, have them begin an initial appointment scenario. The other AEs yell out "Freeze!" if either person is stumbling for words or just if an AE wishes to voice or answer an objection. Let the staff play the game until the second appointment is booked.

Speaker Of The Month

If you want the staff to learn the real language and needs of manufacturers and retailers, invite people from the business community to talk to them. Manufacturer sales reps, broker sales reps and retailer buyers (product, not media) are all good speaker possibilities. Ask your guests to talk about their jobs, the types of promotions that have helped them increase sales, their day-to-day concerns. Allow time for the sales staff to ask questions.

You might want to delegate the sales staff to be in charge of bringing in the monthly speakers. This is a compliment to the speaker and a great "real life" training technique for your staff.

Chapter 27

Taming The "Value-Added" Monster

By Cliff Berkowitz

The Radio community has created a monster, and its name is "added value." But with proper care and nurturing, the added-value monster can be a powerful ally.

The term has become a euphemism for "I want a promotion to go along with my buy or I'm pulling my schedule." As times got tougher in sales, some of the more creative broadcasters started throwing promotions at clients to persuade them to part with their almighty advertising dollars. It worked — unfortunately, too well. Like most things that work in Radio, the rest of the industry followed, and soon "added value" wasn't anything added at all.

- **The value-added monster can be an ally.**
- **Today, programming and sales have conflicting agendas. With more cooperation between departments, stations might tap into a gold mine of promotional opportunities.**
- **Advertisers aren't in the creative promotions business; they only want to sell their product.**
- **Advance planning gives you the opportunity to exploit added-value dollars.**

Like it or not, added value — what we used to call "sales promotion" — is a big part of Radio. Take heart, though. Big-dollar advertisers have big budgets for promotions that can add value to your station's promotions.

Conflicting Agendas, Mediocre Promotions

Back before stations had big promotion budgets (if any), most promotions came from the sales department. Programming would come up with some great idea, then see if sales could get a client to sponsor it. It was generally a win-win situation.

Today, stations are more fragmented, not just formatically but internally. Programming and sales have conflicting promotional agendas, and rarely do they cooperate. This kind of confrontational atmosphere generally leads to mediocre sales promotions that don't get properly sold on the air because programming hates them. When this happens, no one wins. The client loses because the promotion does nothing for them; sales loses because the disappointed client might not continue its relationship with the station. And programming loses because it uses valuable air time with a useless promotion.

Look past this non-productive paradigm and you will see a gold mine of promotional opportunity. While many advertisers have substantial cash to sink into promotions, they aren't in the creative promotions business. They just want to sell their product. If they bring you turnkey promotions, it is likely only as a favor or to ensure that the promotion will be favorable. Most clients are not married to their ready-made promotions. If you can give them something better, they'll love you for it — and you can squeeze more promotional dollars out of them.

Plan Ahead, Get Ahead

The key is to plan ahead. Do your best to map out the year promotionally. Take a day and brainstorm the promotions you want to do. While the promotions department must respond spontaneously to the ever-changing world, there are countless fixed events and holidays you can prepare for. Advance planning gives you the opportunity to exploit added-value dollars. Instead of scrambling for a decent idea, you can have a whole list of promotions from which your clients can choose.

Soon, programming will think of the sales department and clients as allies. If sales is underwriting programming promotions, programming will have more money for other things, or a means of doing promotions when the budget is tight.

No one wins in this game unless everyone wins. This takes planning and teamwork, but it is a healthier way of doing business.

Chapter 28

Determining Your Coverage

By William P. Suffa

"My coverage map contains the entire metro! Ratings are low — something must be wrong with the signal." So starts another long conversation between owner and engineer.

In a previous issue of *Radio Ink*, defining your coverage area and the signal levels necessary for adequate reception were discussed. But defining the coverage area is only half the equation. Computing the size of the coverage area or estimating the strength of the Radio signal is often the most difficult task in predicting coverage. Out of a number of widely accepted methods, each engineer has a favorite, and sometimes these methods show widely varying results.

The methods of predicting FM propagation (signal strength) fall into two categories: general and specific.

General Methods: Easy Calculation, Limited Accuracy

Frequency planners (i.e., FCC and international bodies) do not need to determine where shadowed areas are, the specific signal strengths along major commuter roads or whether advertisers can hear the station. Instead, the FCC needs information on how big the protected coverage area is, whether a large area (the community of license) is in the required contour or whether the main studio is located properly. Any method of computing the coverage of a station that uses generalized information is a general method.

A generalized method has certain advantages: ease of calculation (since you don't need detailed information on the station and surrounding terrain), ability to depict the extent of coverage as a single line (a coverage contour) and ease of defining a protected coverage area for a station. Most U.S. broadcasters' coverage maps are based on a method developed by the FCC. Other general methods include those used by the International Radio Consultative Committee (an arm of the International Telecommunication Union) and the Irregular Terrain Model used by the U.S. Commerce Department's National Telecommunication and Information Administration.

The FCC developed a series of graphs that describe the signal strength at specific distances for the known power of the station and average antenna height above the surrounding countryside. To plot a contour, engineers use these graphs with the power and antenna height above the terrain in at least eight directions from the transmitter site. The distances to a desired signal strength are plotted on a map, and the contour line is drawn to connect them.

There are some pretty big limitations to the FCC's general method. The first is that it averages the terrain for less than 10 miles from the site. If there is a mountain beyond that, tough luck. The second is that it uses the same terrain average regardless of whether the contour falls two miles from the site or 50 miles. Thus, accuracy is limited. (Some, including the FCC, occasionally try to use this method at a greater accuracy than the technique permits. This leads to some incredible results when conducting interference calculations: Rejecting an application for one-tenth mile of interference at 100 miles from the station is like refunding advertiser money for under-running a one-hour program by one second.) Finally, the method does not account for valleys or other shadowed areas.

Specific Methods: Precise But Complex

Specific methods take into account the actual terrain between the transmitter and a given point to predict an actual signal level. The most common techniques are variants of the Longley-Rice terrain limited coverage model and methods described in Technical Note 101, published by the National Bureau of Standards.

Any specific method uses the transmitter data and detailed terrain information (including hills, mountains, valleys, etc.) with a set of statistical formulas to compute the field strength at a given point. The pretty "terrain limited coverage maps" that you can buy are based on calculations made at hundreds of points within the map area.

While more precise than the FCC method, there is a down side to this method. Specific methods are complex and allow many statistical options that can drastically alter the results. The calculations involve substantial computer time and cost. And, worst of all, few engineers agree on the appropriate options to use in any given situation.

If you're comparing two transmitter sites, it is prudent to make sure that the same options and methods were used for each map, or you might make a bad decision. Properly used, however, terrain limited coverage methods are an engineer's best tools to optimize the coverage of a station.

The Dilemma

Different contour levels, different prediction methods, different results. What's a poor owner or manager to do? Use both methods. The FCC method identifies the most reliable coverage area with reasonable results. This is adequate for most sales and financial purposes. Within that coverage area, it makes sense to use a specific terrain limited study to identify trouble areas and optimize coverage. For boosters, terrain limited coverage comparisons are invaluable for determining interference zones.

Of course, if you live in a coverage hole, you may not want to see a terrain limited map. After all, the map might tell you that you can't blame your engineer anymore.

Chapter 29

Stimulating Your Creativity

By Maureen Bulley

- To stimulate your creative ideas, understand what motivates your creativity.
- The Logical Left side of the brain takes care of things like order. The Radical Right is responsible for creativity.
- To manipulate the right side of your brain, first either ignore your left side or take care of its need for order, then address the right side's need for color.
- Know the time of day when you're most creative, and plan to tackle your creative challenges during those hours.

Some people will do just about anything to get a great idea. But why did I have to finish grocery shopping and safely soak my fine washables before I could sit down and write this article?

It's all part of what you know about yourself and what stimulates your creativity. It's how you can succeed at writing account-getting sales proposals and award-winning Radio commercials. This insight is essential, particularly for women. We're sometimes so overwhelmed by our long list of priorities that we don't have time to wait for a great idea to present itself. We have to concentrate on being creative, now.

Whether your challenge is to motivate a sales team or increase your listening audience, you need a creative edge. You need to know what makes you tick. Now, I'm not suggesting you break out the Woolite or head to the corner market ... unless it's been motivational in the past.

Logical Left, Radical Right

The division of labor between right and left brain activities explains why some of the most creative people you know appear to be the most disorganized. This might also explain why some accountants aren't much fun at parties.

The Logical Left side of the brain takes care of things like sequence, numbers and order. The Radical Right is responsible for day-dreaming, color and creativity, to name a few of its delightful qualities.

How, then, do we manipulate the Radical Right side of the brain when we need ideas? Ignore the left, or at least deal with the unanswered correspondence on your desk if you think the sight of it will be distracting.

Next, address the right side's need for color and stimulation. Jot ideas down diagonally on a piece of unruled paper. Use colored pens. Tony Buzan's "Mind-Mapping" techniques are great. Extend lines outward from the central image and build a network of thoughts and ideas on those lines. The result is literally a road map of your mind.

Sleep On It

Germination time is also essential to creativity. This requires absorbing all the facts and actually "sleeping on it." While you're preoccupied with other tasks, the subconscious mind continues to work on your behalf. Some of my greatest "Aha's!" have come while balancing my checkbook.

Just as warming up is essential to physical activity, it's helpful with mental activity as well. Richard Lederer has penned several books that are great for stimulating the brain, including *Crazy English* and *The Play Of Words.*

Make your business office as homey as your home office. Try indirect lighting and pleasing music. And be sure to include some personal items. Seashells or tacky souvenirs from memorable vacations could stimulate the relaxation escape that spawns your next great idea.

Next, ask yourself where you were when you got your last great idea, and duplicate those circumstances. The ideal creative situation for me involves speeding down the highway with the stereo cranked up.

Negative Stress Vs. Positive Energy

While deadlines can impose negative stress, they can also create positive energy. Use self-imposed deadlines if you must, particularly if you're the type who performs best under pressure. Know the time of day when you're most creative, and plan to tackle creative challenges during those hours.

Whether your application of creativity is to write better scripts and presentations or to develop new promotions and marketing strategies, you need to tap your creativity promptly. If you're like me, that means getting that grocery shopping and laundry out of the way, and waiting until the deadline looms over your head like a bad haircut.

Chapter 30

Characteristics Of Good Decision-Making

Decide And Conquer

By Rick Ott

There are as many different management styles as there are people in management. But despite the differences, all good managers share common characteristics.

One common trait is the ability to make decisions quickly and confidently. Conversely, managers who have trouble making decisions, or who doubt themselves after making one, seem to be running troubled operations.

Honing your decision-making skills always pays off. Here are four characteristics of good decision-making. Adopt these four, and you're way ahead of most.

- **Most good managers make important decisions in collaboration with one other person.**
- **No more than two people should be part of a decision. The more people involved, the longer it takes to reach a decision.**
- **Good managers make decisions with limited information, acknowledging there's no such thing as total certainty.**
- **To make a decision, good managers eliminate their options in rapid order.**
- **Delegate decision-making as far down the line as possible. By empowering their people to make decisions, good managers become great managers.**

It Takes Two

Operate in two-person decision-making teams. Most good managers make important decisions in collaboration with one other person. Two-person decision-making teams, who decide by consensus, work extremely well in most cases.

Why are there two and only two pilots in each jet? Discussion aids decision-making, and you need at least two people to discuss. And if one person misses something or makes an error, the other can catch it. Also, one outranks the other. When an important, snap decision must be made, there's no time to debate who's in charge.

Too Many Cooks

If two-person decision-making teams work well, why not put three, four or more people into the mix? Weak managers seem to like that idea. They like to bring as many people into the decision-making arena as they can find. I've seen some stations with as many as seven or eight people involved in every decision, from what the spring promotion will be to how the logo should look.

When you start adding more decision-makers, all kinds of problems develop. First, debates rage on and on. The more people involved, the longer it takes to reach a decision. Second, decision by committee means compromise. And compromise almost always means a weakened, watered-down plan. Third, group dynamics proliferate. People express opinions and take sides to make themselves look good or to play politics. There's always someone who vetoes an idea just to be separate from the crowd.

Keep Moving

Good managers make decisions with limited information, acknowledging there's no such thing as total certainty. They gather some information, then make assumptions and decisions based on their assumptions. They know it's better to be deciding and moving, with limited information, than sitting idle, awaiting certainty.

Poor managers spend an inordinate amount of time gathering information, researching to death. They fail to realize that more and more information offers less and less value. And the more information you gather, the more evenly your alternatives weigh out, making it that much harder to decide. While these managers spend time info-gorging, opportunity windows are constantly passing them by.

Fewer Options, More Power

To make a decision, good managers eliminate their options in rapid order, eventually having one remaining option that becomes their chosen course of action. They understand that by cutting off possibilities, they are empowering themselves greatly by moving ahead quickly and decisively.

Weak managers are forever trying to "hold their options open." They are afraid to eliminate any options, because they see that as weakening their position. They fail to realize that too many options are actually a heavy sedative. As a result, they remain at the fork in the road, spending their valuable time debating which road to take, instead of moving.

Decide By Delegating

Good managers delegate decision-making down the ranks, as far down the line as possible. And they don't chastise people when they make a mistake. By empowering people to make decisions, good managers become great managers.

Poor managers are afraid to delegate. They require even the smallest of decisions be "run by me" for approval. Driven by insecurity, poor managers make sure nothing happens without their OK. As a consequence, not much does happen. And the talent, creativity and brain power of others remains shamefully underutilized.

Chapter 31

AM Coverage

The Sky's The Limit

By William P. Suffa

- **Defining AM coverage is more complex than for FM.**
- **Groundwave coverage is considered both day and night, while skywave coverage may be used at night.**
- **For clear channel stations, skywave service can extend 650 miles or more.**
- **Measured and estimated ground conductivities can produce drastic differences in coverage maps.**

Nothing is simple when it comes to AM Radio stations. With directional antennas, differences between the daytime and nighttime coverage (and interference), large antenna and ground systems, seasonal coverage changes, noise — well, you get the idea — it's difficult to make a buck.

Merely trying to explain the coverage — and coverage maps — is significantly more complicated than with FM. Forget the matter of audience: If you can't explain your coverage to advertisers or bankers, you can't sell the station.

Night And Day

Unlike FM signals, which generally travel within a line of sight from the transmitter, AM signals travel in two different modes: groundwave and skywave. During nighttime hours, both modes are considered when evaluating the coverage of an AM station. In the daytime, coverage is generally defined by the groundwave signal, because the effect of skywave is negligible. During the transition between day and night (normal people call it dusk, Radio engineers call it "critical hours"), groundwave signals provide reliable Radio coverage, while skywave signals merely result in interference to that coverage.

OK, so what is groundwave coverage? And what is skywave?

With groundwave coverage, the soil acts like a big wire, conducting Radio signals along the Earth's surface between transmitter and receiver. That is the reason a good ground system (and proper siting of the antenna) is vital. The conductivity of the soil varies, depending on the weather, climate, region and season, but those changes generally occur over long periods of time (weeks or months).

If you look in the FCC's Rules for AM stations (you do have a copy of the Rules, don't you?), you will see a map of the United States (labeled M-3 or R-3) which describes the estimated conductivity for various parts of the country. The higher the number, the better the conductivity, and the farther groundwave signals travel.

Note that I said estimated. The FCC prepared this map decades ago using measurements on some AM stations and geological analysis of the soil in various regions of the country. The actual ground conductivity in many areas of the United States varies significantly from the FCC's estimates. It is, however, much easier for an engineer to use estimated values from the FCC's map, or a computerized representation of the map, than it is to determine and use measured values. It's probably worth a discussion with your engineer to ensure that the soil conductivity values used to prepare your coverage maps are appropriate.

Distant Wavelengths

Skywave signals propagate more like FM signals, except that AM signals are of such long wavelength that they bounce off various layers of the atmosphere and fall to Earth at long distances from the transmitter. For clear channel stations, nighttime skywave coverage can reach 650 miles or more, although directional antennas may limit the coverage in the home market. (I remember one station that had an internal slogan about its coverage: "Five states, three countries and parts of the Capital metro.")

Although random, hourly atmospheric changes prevent us from precisely computing the signal strength at any given time, there are enough long-term data for engineers to predict the impact of skywave signals on a statistical basis. The FCC specifies a particular method to calculate such signals. Using a formula leaves far less room to manipulate skywave signal strength figures.

A Crowded Band

Predicting and defining the actual coverage for AM stations seems to be an inexact science. And maybe the lack of good planning (by stuffing too many stations into the band) has contributed to the AM coverage and interference problem. There is plenty of blame to go around, but the wide skywave service areas are the chief culprit. This problem will remain second to none until (or unless) satellite-based transmission systems reach general acceptance. And, on a good receiver, some stations sound really great.

Now, if I could only fix the listener perceptions about the bad quality of AM Radio …

Chapter 32

Man Handling In Negotiations

Myths About The Male Animal

By Mimi Donaldson

Most of the women I've worked with in corporate America regard themselves as good communicators. And, for the most part, they are. But when it comes to the art of negotiating, I've noticed that men are better at it. Over the past 20 years, through observation only, I have concluded that: a) negotiating is a game, b) men have played games and competed longer than we have and c) they are more experienced and, hence, more skilled at negotiating. Besides, they have testosterone, that nasty ol' male hormone that makes them aggressive.

Myth No. 1:
Men already respect you.

Myth No. 2:
Men are complex creatures.

Myth No. 3:
Talking it out will solve the problem.

Myth No. 4:
When men say "uh-huh," they are encouraging you to talk more.

Myth No. 5:
When men talk about themselves, they're not interested in you.

Myth No. 6:
Men know how to be and will be good losers.

Myth No. 7:
Men believe in win-win negotiations.

"Know your opponent" is the rule of any good competition. And any good negotiation. We women get into trouble when we assume (and you know what "assume" does) that we can talk to a man in a negotiation exactly the way we talk to a woman. And it's just not true. To negotiate from a basis of strength — whether in selling Radio spots or going after that general manager's position — you need to know: Who are these people called men and where are they coming from? For that reason, I give you my Seven Deadly Myths women have about men which are wrong, wrong, wrong.

Your Mother Was Wrong

You must dispel the following myths to become good negotiators:

Myth No. 1: Men already respect you. Wrong. You must earn their respect right at the negotiating table. Never assume your credentials preceded you and that your background, education, brilliant maneuvers in the Radio industry have established you before you walked in the door. Picture in your mind the male negotiator behind a big desk, clean surface, his eyes glittering, his hands clasped, saying: "So! Tell me why you should get my ad!" He wants to play, and the game starts now. Every sentence out of your mouth has to sell yourself or your station, in some way building your credibility and respect in his eyes. This is not bragging, and even if it is, it's OK — your mother was wrong.

Myth No. 2: Men are complex creatures. They are not — women are. Men are very simple people — not stupid — simple. They mean what they say, and they say what they mean — very few hidden meanings. They like their communications short, to the point. Give them bullets, a one-paragraph summary of your conclusions.

Tell them how long it will take, and don't go over the allotted time. Men like to "set their energy clocks," and they don't like to run out of energy. They are afraid to run out of energy; it puts them out of control. And, as we know, that makes them cranky.

Solve The Problem

Myth No. 3: Talking it out will solve the problem. Wrong. Men think most long, drawn-out talking actually confuses the issue and creates problems. Women say "let's talk it out" and men start to shift in their seats. They want to get right to the point. They don't want to talk "about" the problem; they just want to solve it. Or, as a former boss of mine used to say, to the chagrin of all of us: "Spare me the delivery. Just give me the baby!"

Myth No. 4: When men say "uh-huh," they are encouraging you to talk more. No. It's true for women. We interject sounds and non-words to draw people out. We mean "keep talking." When a man is interested, he is silent, looking at you, focused. When he says "uh-huh," he means wrap it up, now. His energy clock is winding down.

Listen And Learn

Myth No. 5: When men talk about themselves, they're not interested in you. True about women, not men. When women dominate the conversation, talking only of themselves, they're not interested in you. But men are sharing themselves, and are grateful for a female listener who listens attentively. If you let him "hold forth," you learn a lot (an advantage in negotiation) and you gain points for being a good listener.

Myth No. 6: Men know how to be and will be good losers. They will say they do. They made up the phrase: "It's not whether you win or lose — it's how you play the game." That phrase hangs over every Olympic Game. Don't believe it. Even at the Olympics, gracious losing is not in vogue. Winning is the only fun. Losing causes men to lose face, and they hate that most of all.

Myth No. 7: Men believe in win-win negotiations. No. It's a popularly held concept, but it goes against their genes. It's win-lose. That's the only way they play. Women are far too concerned about the other guy's welfare in a negotiation. Let him take care of himself. You don't have to make it nice for everyone. That's not your job. Your job is to get what you want.

Chapter 33

Cable Poses Challenges For Radio

No Idle Threats

By Michael H. Bader

- **The threat by cable to Radio broadcasters is real. Cable can get moving with digital long before the on-air stations.**
- **Cable has no ownership limit on how many channels it can provide.**
- **Cable is likely to treat Radio the same it did TV, by dropping any commercial stations in favor of their own programming.**
- **The smart broadcaster will sew up cable channels and become a partner with the local cable company.**

The cable company in Maryland's Montgomery County is pitching its cable Radio: "Continuous music! No raspy disc jockeys! No annoying commercials! Soon you may hear this sound round the clock!" And "this sound" is digital, clear and pretty professional.

The threat to Radio broadcasters is real. It is immediate. Cable can get moving with digital long before the on-air stations. While the industry studies digital and the accompanying satellite stations, cable will go ahead and render the service.

The scope of the threat is magnified. Cable has no ownership limit on how many channels it can provide. It can format everything from rock to Bach. It can provide multiple offerings within a format.

And the threat is aggravated by the possibility that cable providers will eventually drop any commercial FM stations that they currently carry in favor of their own programming. Cable will no longer be content with offering an array of local stations, some powerhouse from distant markets and a Muzak type of its own. Cable can remove all of these and do all of the programming by itself.

The promise of commercial-free programming is illusory. We all heard the cable promise of enhanced picture quality from existing television stations years ago. Now, more often than we care to experience, cable is dropping the existing stations and adding its own pay channels.

Some of Radio broadcasting's allies are targeted to become part of the Radio cable effort. More than one national rep is staffing and planning for the day when these so-called commercial-free Radio services are laden with their own spots. It has to happen.

Well, what of Radio's unique feature of automobile reception? Can cable penetrate that? Probably so, since cable is looking hard and long at the new Personal Communications Service (PCS) that will go anywhere the vehicle goes. Cable is smart enough to realize that one can program on such a medium just as well as it can carry voice or paging or dispatching. PCS, therefore, is not just a substitute for cellular or Marti communications. It promises a variety of audio purposes, and one could be music, news, sports and the like. If you want to experience the functional equivalent of this, listen to the new on-board airliner services from such groups as In-Flight. Soon you could be hearing the same in your car.

Embrace, Ally, Re-Examine

With this threat, what is Radio to do? First, broadcasters must embrace — not dread — the arrival of digital. That digital purity of sound is going to be the standard. Local stations, therefore, must take the plunge into digital. Second, alliances with the local cable system might be the answer. Bearing in mind that the FCC still pretty well restricts to four the number of audio outlets for one group (two AM and two FM) in a market, Radio broadcasters can always have as many cable channels as they please. The smart broadcaster, therefore, is going to sew up cable channels, become a "partner" with the local cable company and operate in that medium as well as over the air.

Third, broadcasters should re-examine the commercial load, the level of talk and other essential characteristics of their business to determine how to change. It will be hard to compete with commercial-free cable music. (If there is any doubt, think back to the many newcomers in markets around the nation that started FM stations with so many weeks of commercial-free programming to storm into the ratings books. That's exactly what cable is going to do.) There's no way to stop this trend, so Radio broadcasters must improve service, get into the new medium and compete fully on their own terms.

Is this really serious? The government thinks so. It recently added to its rules and policies implementing the 1992 Cable Act a provision of re-transmission consent payments for Radio as well as television signals. It would not be prudent to add a profit factor to the 1993 financial statement for some extra money for this item, but down the line Radio stations just may find a few additional dollars from this source. So, if the government thinks it prudent to include in the cable rules a re-transmission consent (that is, dollars) for Radio on cable, there just may be something to this thesis.

Chapter 34

Get Backup

And Stay On The Air

By Roy Pressman

How often does your station go off the air? Lengthy and numerous off-air times reduce revenue and hurt your station's ratings, but common sense and a few wisely spent dollars can keep that from happening.

How many backup systems are installed at your facility? Frequent technical failures indicate that you need to look at your station's redundant systems. Your facility should have backup systems in the studio, STL link and transmitter site. These systems provide alternate means of broadcasting when your main systems fail.

- **Off-air times reduce revenue and affect your station's ratings.**
- **Have a second studio that can easily go on air when your air studio has problems.**
- **Many stations back up their STL microwave links with equalized telephone circuits.**
- **The backup transmitter doesn't have to be a Cadillac, just reliable.**
- **Back up your antenna system by mounting a one- or two-bay antenna and feed line system somewhere on your tower.**
- **Be prepared in the event of power failures by having a generator on hand to supply emergency power to essential areas.**

A Second Studio

Your air studio should be able to function even if you lose a cart machine, a CD player or a microphone. Just make sure the studio is equipped with at least two functioning microphones, three cart machines and three CD players. This configuration will prevent panic and possible loss of revenue when there are failures. In addition, it's a good idea to have a second studio (it could be a production room) that can easily go on the air in the event your air studio has serious problems, such as a mixing console failure.

Alternate Links

If your studios are not collocated with your transmitter site, your station is using some form of studio transmitter link (STL). It's either a microwave link or a system utilizing equalized telephone lines. Both systems are usually extremely reliable, but you should have an alternate system that will keep you on the air when your main STL fails. Many stations back up their STL microwave links with equalized telephone circuits. This gives you two entirely separate paths from your studio to your transmitter site.

If you prefer a redundant microwave system, manufacturers such as Moseley and TFT have interfaces that can detect problems and automatically switch to the backup system in the event of a failure. Check with your engineer to see how long it would take to get your backup STL system on the air (ask if you have a backup first!). Remember, when your STL goes down, you're off the air.

The Trusty Transmitter

It's good engineering practice to have some type of backup transmitter. Stations without a backup will be faced with hours and possibly days of off-air time. The backup transmitter doesn't have to be a Cadillac, in fact it doesn't need the same power output as your main transmitter, but it should be reliable and easy to put on the air. Test the backup weekly, either on the air or into a dummy load. Look into automatic systems that can put your backup transmitter on the air in the event your main transmitter fails.

If your transmitter site relies on air conditioning for cooling, make sure there are two air conditioners and make sure that each one by itself can handle the heat load produced by the transmitter. You are going to feel pretty silly if an air conditioner failure takes you off the air. Believe it or not, a transmitter in a sealed room with no air conditioning can raise the room temperature to over 130 degrees.

Remote Possibilities

The remote control system allows you to control your transmitter site from your studio. If it fails, you may be required to go off the air or send an operator to your transmitter site until it is repaired. To avoid this dilemma, purchase an additional remote control system to act as a backup. Have your engineer wire it in parallel with the main unit.

Auxiliary Antenna

We take our reliable antenna systems for granted, but they can and do fail. It's not uncommon for FM stations to be off the air for many days because of an antenna or transmission line failure. It takes time to fly in parts or a new antenna, and the tower crew must make the repairs.

A smart solution is to mount a one- or two-bay antenna and associated transmission line at some height on your tower. Don't be too picky about height; this is an emergency antenna that will keep you on the air until you can repair your main antenna system. Install a patch panel or coaxial switch arrangement in your transmitter facility. This will allow you to quickly change over to your backup antenna system when problems arise.

Another Source Of Power

One of the most common causes of off-air time is lack of juice from the power company. If you can't live with the interruptions, install a backup generator at your studio and transmitter site. You can keep the studio generator size and cost to a minimum by feeding emergency power only to essential areas: studios and associated equipment, overhead lighting, telephone systems and studio air conditioners.

The generator at the transmitter site should be able to power your main transmitter and any associated equipment at full power. Select a fuel storage tank that will give you at least two days of emergency power. Don't forget to check the fuel level in your tank occasionally. Typical storage tanks can hold from 500 to 2,000 gallons. Test your generators weekly and conduct semiannual preventive maintenance.

Audio Processing

It doesn't matter where you install your audio processing equipment (at your studio or transmitter site), but make sure you have a backup system ready to go on the air. A great backup FM audio processor is the Orban Optimod 8000A. It hasn't been made for quite a few years, but it sounds good, is reliable and sells for about $1,500 on the used market. This is money well-spent.

When In Doubt, Check It Out

Each time you go off the air, talk to your engineer and find out what happened. Ask how you can prevent future failures. Be supportive and budget the necessary funds to install backup systems in all critical areas. If you've done your homework, your station will stay on the air.

Chapter 35

Intimate Vs. Instrumental

Communicating For Love And Money

By Dr. Sharon Crain

- **Men have been trained to excel in the work arena: women have learned to excel in the social or love arena.**
- **As a result, men have focused on a style of communicating — instrumental — appropriate for creating money; women have focused on the intimate style of communicating, appropriate for creating love.**
- **People often get into trouble when they carry over a style appropriate for one arena into the other.**
- **To maintain a balance, it is necessary to envision yourself as having two different parts: the intimate part and the instrumental part.**

Historically, men have gone off to hunt, to sea, to war, to explore. Our culture has trained them to develop a set of competitive skills of economic value. In other words, men have been trained to excel in the work arena.

As women, we historically have kept the home fires burning and have been trained to develop a set of intimate relationship skills of social value. We have learned to excel in the social arena — the arena of love.

As a result of these historical differences, men and women have focused on two different styles of communicating and relating — one appropriate for creating money and one appropriate for creating love. Let's look at some of the differences between these two communication styles and learn how to communicate for love *and* money.

In the arena of work, the overall purpose of communicating is to accomplish results for your Radio station. In fact, work relationships are task-oriented and involve the exchange of data and information in order to produce a specific result. This style of communicating is termed instrumental.

By contrast, in the social arena, the purpose of relating is to self-express. Communications focus on the expression of emotions, feelings and personal fulfillment. This manner of communicating and relating in the social arena is termed intimate.

The structure of the relationship is another major difference. Instrumental relationships are highly structured, as evidenced by organizational charts, job descriptions and specific procedures. This same kind of structure and inflexibility applied to a social or love relationship would probably end it!

Separating Work And Love

We often get into trouble when we carry over a style that is appropriate for one arena into the other. We are all familiar with the stereotypical husband who is stuck in the instrumental style of relating. When his working wife wants to share frustrations over a day in which the car stalled, the dishwasher died, the baby sitter was late and she had an important meeting with her biggest advertiser — he tells her to call the mechanic and the plumber and find a new baby sitter.

Women find the same problem when we enter the work world. Traditionally, we may be so used to communicating with friends and family in the intimate style that it is difficult to learn to communicate instrumentally. Often, we see examples of women who have never learned to relate instrumentally, such as the woman sales manager who "mothers" her salespeople. Rather than manage performance, she nurtures personalities. At the opposite extreme are women who have adopted the instrumental style with such a vengeance that they find it difficult to build appropriate business relationships.

An important challenge for the modern working couple is to avoid turning the love arena into an extension of the work arena, and vice versa. If you fill every weekend with goals, tasks and projects, where every waking moment is planning and nothing is spontaneous, you are in danger of losing the very thing the majority of men and women say they want most — a loving, intimate relationship.

To maintain a balance, it is necessary to envision yourself as having two different parts: the intimate part, appropriate for your social self, and the instrumental part, appropriate for your professional self.

To accomplish this, you need to first create self-awareness — to pay attention and notice your present style. Notice, for example, if you find yourself using only one of the styles both at work and at home.

This circumstance tends to be more common in men who have never recognized that there is more than the instrumental style. In seminars, I have seen men practically in tears say: "I want to relate to my partner in a way that is meaningful to her — but how do I do it?"

If you are a partner in this situation, explain in an instrumental style about the two different styles to create the awareness. Then, it is important to refocus on the very purpose of intimate communication — which is to openly express feelings and emotions in a safe environment.

As women, your personal challenge is to remember that you can enhance your professional relationships in the economic arena without having to abandon your intimate role in the social arena. In other words, you can have both love and money.

Chapter 36

A Foot In The Door

Word To Wise Job-Seekers

By Bill Burton

Don't know about you, but I'm constantly asked by friends, family and clients to talk to some young person who is trying to find their way into the communications or advertising business. Most I interview have no real-world direction on how to pursue a job. At best, they've had a two-hour course on how to write a resume which is, as far as I'm concerned, one of the least important ingredients in getting a job.

- **Develop a verbal and written presentation.**
- **Practice your presentation. Even better, videotape it and have someone critique it.**
- **During the interview, make eye-to-eye contact and let your prospects know you want the job.**
- **Follow up the interview with a personal letter.**

For those reasons, I've put together the following plan. It's a little bit of payback for all the fabulous times I've had in this great business. You may want to share my road map with some of the young people who come to your door.

Know Where You're Going

When looking for a job, you must have a plan, be prepared and be doggedly persistent.

1.) Determine what profession you want to pursue. Hopefully, the courses you took in college have at least partially predetermined this direction.

In our particular business, Radio salespeople come from a variety of curriculums. From my experience, the following may well be the most desirable degrees: business/economics; telecommunications; advertising; journalism; speech/English.

2.) Target an industry. If you want to be in Radio sales, pick out 12

Radio stations within a given area and pre-search them. By pre-search, I mean, prior to ever contacting the stations, find out as much as you can about them.

3.) Develop a verbal and written presentation. Let your prospective employer know why you will be an asset to their company.

Dress Rehearsal

4.) Practice your presentation. Practice in front of your family, a friend and the mirror.

If you have access to video equipment, tape your presentation and then critique yourself? Do you look eager to go to work? Ask someone you respect to critique the tape with you.

In addition to leaving or sending a resume, why not a short, well-done video on yourself? I've had hundreds of people send me a resume; no one has ever sent me a personal pitch on tape.

5.) Set up appointments, preferably by phone. If that does not work, ask in writing for an appointment. If that does not succeed, possibly an overnight wire. If that strikes out, go directly to that station without an appointment and keep going back and back again.

People love to be pursued and love to help people. So, providing you're not abrasive, chances are the more you pursue them, the more they'll want to help you.

6.) Prior to the interview, re-study your pre-search. Rehearse your presentation.

7.) Actual Interview. Eye-to-eye contact is imperative. State why you're there, then give your presentation on why you would be a benefit to the company.

Be forthright and direct. Let them know that you're not there just to be interviewed, but you want the job. Ask very directly: "May I have the job? ... When can I start?"

If you are given a definite "no," ask: "When can I check back?" Ask if there is more information you can give them and what they are looking for in the people they hire.

Follow Up

At this point, listen well. Take a pad of paper along to take notes. Taking notes demonstrates to them that you're conscientious and are eager to learn.

After the interview and prior to leaving, give them a copy of your presentation on why you want to work for them. Also leave a one-page resume. They might insist that you give them your resume early on, but it is best to make your presentation first.

8.) After the interview, follow up with a personal letter going over the benefits of why you want to work for the Radio station. Conclude the letter with a forthright request to go to work for them. Always ask for the order.

The Payoff Of Perseverance

9.) P-E-R-S-I-S-T-E-N-C-E. Remember, frequency sells. The average salesperson makes three calls and quits. The average sale is made after the third call. Make up your mind that the job is yours and persevere.

You may think these suggestions are a bit trite or beneath you, but I can tell you firsthand that they have influenced some of the biggest people in American industry.

As a recent example, a friend's nephew used my direction and went on to get a job at Bozell Inc. After he got the job, they informed him that 43 people were pursuing the position. He got the job because of his perseverance.

10.) Opportunity is more important than income. Go for the opportunity, and the money will follow. My dad taught us: "Do more than what you get paid for, and you'll soon get paid more for what you're doing."

Chapter 37

Some Tips On Coverage

And The Difference Between Night And Day

By William P. Suffa

In the past few days, I have been rebuilding two AM directional Radio stations.

I was brought face-to-face with two antenna systems which — because of poor designs or deterioration — were not radiating as much power as they could. Unlike FM stations, AM antenna systems (particularly directional antennas) can be misadjusted in a way that severely reduces coverage.

- **AM coverage is affected by the ground conditions and seasonal variations.**
- **AM nighttime coverage is limited by interference from other stations.**
- **Poor coverage may be an indicator of antenna system problems.**

Acceptable Coverage Defined

The FCC defines several levels of acceptable coverage, depending on the class of station, the interference constraints, daytime and nighttime operation and whether or not the intended audience is in rural or urban areas.

For clear channel stations (Class I and A), there is significant, wide-area coverage within the groundwave (reliable) and skywave (intermittent) service areas. For other classes of stations, the only protected coverage is the groundwave coverage during daytime and nighttime hours.

Daytime Coverage

During daytime hours, the FCC considers the coverage area of a non-clear channel AM station to be within the 0.5 contour. For clear channel stations, coverage is assumed to be within the 0.1 mV/m contour. These contours are normally shown on an AM station coverage map. The smaller 2 mV/m contour is not generally shown.

The significance of 2 mV/m is simply this: Noise levels are higher in urban and suburban areas, and AM signals are susceptible to interference from electrical noise. Based on many studies, the FCC has established 2 mV/m as being adequate for interference-free service in urban/suburban areas. Realistically, however, the "city grade," or 5 mV/m, contour better defines coverage in areas with tall buildings, dense overhead wires and major underpasses.

The 0.5 mV/m (or 0.1 mV/m, as appropriate) contour provides only a marginal representation of the service area, except in rural situations. Even there, noise and electrical interference will degrade the AM signal. The 0.5 mV/m contour sure looks bigger than the 2 mV/m contour on the map, and sales is a game of perception. Because of some old FCC policies designed to encourage placement of AM stations in small towns, not all stations are fully protected to the 0.5 mV/m and 0.1 mV/m contours.

Nighttime Coverage

Here's where it really gets interesting. Skywave signals can either provide coverage or service, or cause interference to the groundwave coverage of certain stations.

Clear channel stations are protected by the FCC to provide both reliable nighttime groundwave service to the 0.5 mV/m contour, and intermittent (or secondary) service to the 0.5 mV/m skywave contour. The skywave service contour is predicted using a statistical premise that the signal will be available half the time. Although actual reception may occur beyond those contours (and reception may be impaired within those contours), the 0.5 mV/m groundwave and skywave contours are the extent of a clear channel nighttime coverage area. Not that it's all that shabby: A typical non-directional clear channel station will provide secondary nighttime service to a radius of about 650 miles from the transmitter. For directional clear channel stations, the skywave contour is calculated in an iterative procedure using the actual power in each direction along with the FCC skywave prediction formula.

That's easy enough. Regional local channels are a different story altogether. The nighttime service of these stations results in the greatest problems of interference, and is most lacking in suitable coverage.

Why? Because the effective coverage is limited to the area that does not receive interference from other stations at night. This is called "Nighttime Interference-Free" coverage. According to the FCC, the nighttime interference-free coverage is determined by computing the amount of interference received from other stations using a method called Root Sum Square. This RSS value is called the "night limit," which simply means that coverage is limited at night to the area inside the RSS value coverage contour.

The station signals go as far as they do in daytime, but the actual coverage contour is only at the higher "limited" signal level. It is interference that limits nighttime coverage more than anything else. In many cases, the night coverage is barely adequate to serve the community of license.

What Does It All Mean?

It means that you should ask your engineer a lot of questions when preparing coverage maps. What can you do? Ask what assumptions were made, and what procedures were used. Drive the signal. See if the assumptions "seem" right. We all know: "If you can't hear it, you can't sell it." But remember, in many parts of the country, the coverage varies with the season. Also, remember that poor coverage may be the result of antenna system deterioration or design problems.

Chapter 38

Hiring Winners

Prevention! Detection! Correction!

By Dave Gifford

- **The problem is not how we pay salespeople, it's who we're paying.**
- **Hiring errors come from hiring only when we have to hire.**
- **Ongoing recruiting is a must!**
- **Hiring without testing costs you thousands and thousands of dollars yearly.**
- **Prevention and detection eliminate correction.**

There is a great hue and cry throughout Radioland that we're paying our salespeople wrong. Wrong!

Given that 20 percent of most sales staffs should be fired, with at least another 20 percent suspended in a kind of free-floating purgatory zone for low to mid plodders, the problem isn't how we're paying, it's who we're paying. Face it, any number of existing compensation formulas would suffice, however dated, if you hired the right salespeople in the first place. Compensation plans don't sell anything.

Eventually everybody will leave your station for one reason or another, including you. So, depending on how long you hang around, you will always have more salespeople to hire and, regretfully, more salespeople to fire. That's the nature of this business.

Turnover becomes a problem, however, only if you hire too quickly and fire too late. Then, you can't blame your hired-fired problems on the volatile nature of the Radio industry, can you, because the problem is you. Proving once again that all sales problems are sales management problems.

Prevention! Detection! Correction! That's my formula for eliminating problems. But it is especially useful in eliminating hiring errors. For the purpose of this particular chapter, let's confine our attention to prevention and detection only.

Recruiting Quality

Question: What are you doing to eliminate hiring errors? Two suggestions …

1.) Every single day, without exception, until your interviews and testing uncover no fewer than three winning candidates, run the following ad in your local newspaper's classifieds:

"Currently there are no openings for sales executives at (call letters). However, if you are driven to be the best and want to be paid best, then we want to talk to you about your future, now. Only qualified candidates will be interviewed, and all former employers will be contacted. Please send cover letter and resume to (your name/call letters/address). E.O.E."

Who will not respond to the above ad? Unemployed salespeople (for good reasons) and anyone else not willing to stand the test of you contacting their former employers.

Who will respond to the above ad? Employed salespeople (for good reasons), self-motivated salespeople, salespeople who get up in the morning for their careers and not for a job and anyone else confident enough to risk even the most critical reference reviews.

Please note that you will not receive the number of responses you might be accustomed to from classified advertising, because the purpose of the above ad is to yield quality, not quantity. Patience!

What I'm suggesting is that recruiting must become a continuing process, and that your purpose should be to build a farm system — stable, if you will — of self-motivated, success-driven individuals who would kill to sell for your station at the first opportunity.

A Ready List Of Winners

Let's now fast-forward to that day when you have to either fire someone or someone quits. All you have to do, keeping in mind that all three finalists are pre-selected winners, is to pick up the phone, go down your prioritized list of candidates and, one by one, call until you come up with a winner. Now what? Re-order the above classified ad (maybe this time under "Business Opportunities" rather than "Sales Agents") and run same, every single day without a break, until your interviews and testing uncover no fewer than three more winners for your ready list.

2.) Testing? Testing!

Today, if I were back running Radio stations, I would not hire a single salesperson without testing, period. Not all your candidates, mind you, only your short list of finalists.

But, I can hear you say, you're not convinced those testing companies are all that accurate, right? Welcome to the 1990s. Witness …

A couple of years ago, to prove their accuracy to one of my New Zealand clients, I secured a free test from one of two testing companies I most often recommend to my stations. Very smartly, the sales manager tested a salesperson on her staff whom she knew, as the saying goes, like the back of her hand, and the test results revealed a mirror-perfect copy of that individual. However, the last line in the testing company's report warned that the tested individual might be considering a career move at that particular time. The next day, said tested individual turned in his resignation to go to work for a competing Radio station.

The lesson is that if you budget for on-going recruiting (Prevention!) and testing (Detection!), maybe you won't need Correction!

Chapter 39

Document Everything

Or You Could Face A Wrongful Termination Suit

By Chris Gable

Think of the last time you were involved in an employer vs. employee dispute. If you have enough distance from the conflict, perhaps you can reflect on what occurred, why it occurred and how the entire situation could have been avoided.

Chances are that your view today is much more objective than it was when the dispute took place. You might even see things from the opposite point of view. With that power in hand, let's explore how documentation can, in many cases, help you avoid a wrongful termination and discrimination lawsuit.

- **Your notes, documented correspondence and meetings could save you in wrongful termination or discrimination suits.**
- **There must be a clear policy stating the nature of evaluations and that evaluations will be given frequently and routinely.**
- **Documentation, frequent meetings, regular evaluations and clear, honest communication with employees are vital to station operations.**

Self-Destructing Dream

In the summer of 1992, the station hired "Jane," an attractive, perky, afternoon drive personality. Everything about her seemed right. Her show was appealing, her knack for public appearances was selling remotes and — best of all — she did not cost a lot of money. As a bonus, she performed with little or no direction — a manager's and PD's dream employee ... not!

What took place over the following six months should convince anyone that documentation, frequent meetings, regular evaluations and clear, honest communication with employees are vital to station operations.

Since Jane required little or no direction, her PD met with her infrequently at first and even less as time went on. Because her show and remote work were above average and had sales appeal, management showcased and pampered her, making her feel special. Besides, the station management felt the extra attention would make up for the low salary … Wrong!

What the station did not count on was her growing need for money. She shared an apartment with one of the station's part-timers, but expenses were high and getting higher. Her bills were backing up and tension was mounting. Jane was about to begin a long period of self-destruction.

Mounting Doubts

First, Jane began to doubt her performance. She asked her PD for a critique, but he was too busy and told her: "You sound fine, just relax." Jane began to lose interest in her show — a little less show prep here, a missed break there — and within a very short time Jane had reason to doubt her performance. It was terrible, and she wasn't the only one who noticed. Her fellow staffers heard the difference too, but didn't feel right saying anything. So all remained quiet.

About a month later, Jane actually missed a remote. Actually, she never really knew about it; she didn't see the slip of paper in her mailbox describing the remote in handwritten scrawl. Monday morning, the meeting with the PD brought tears, apologies and protests.

The meeting ended with Jane taking the blame but not believing she was wrong. Her distrust continued to build when her request for a raise was denied for budget reasons. "We'll talk later," her bosses told her.

Soon Jane was a classic problem employee. She came to work only in the nick of time, doing only what was required and soon began to turn down remotes and appearances that were above her weekly hours.

By now, everyone believed that Jane should be replaced, and the PD was the one to do it. In fact, he even began to document her every mistake. Finally, he pulled the plug and on Friday afternoon told Jane she was finished.

No Documents, No Defense

Imagine everyone's shock three weeks later when they were notified that Jane had filed a wrongful termination and discrimination suit. She charged that she was singled out, that no one else had undergone such rigorous examination of their performance. She noted her own performance had not been evaluated until she "embarrassed" the PD with the missed remote, which she defended by saying she hadn't been notified.

During the trial, the station management strongly contested the point regarding lack of documentation and evaluation. However, there were no notes on any employee except Jane, and those notes did not begin until after the disputed remote. There were no formal evaluations other than the yearly reviews which had not come up yet, because they were always done in April.

It should be no surprise that Jane won her case and was awarded a substantial amount of cash. And imagine the PD's shock when he got his walking papers because he allowed the whole thing to happen.

Who is to blame? Let's start from the top down. Each evaluation must include a written statement that is shared and discussed in detail with the employee, as well as a detailed program and timetable for any necessary improvements.

Constructive Contact

Station management must implement the program at all levels, instructing department heads to meet with staff on at least a weekly basis. If properly documented, these weekly meetings can serve as performance evaluations. Praise for exceptional work, suggestions for improving poor work and support for making good work great can be noted at each meeting and provide details of each employee's progress or failure.

Regular and frequent contact will guarantee that an employee feels able to communicate, and it will break the barrier that often builds between reluctant managers and quiet employees.

Train department heads in proper employee relations and documentation. Yes, the PD was to blame for much of the problem with Jane, but how well-informed was he in the first place? How well had management trained him for his role as a department head? His tenure as the "best jock" was not, in itself, a qualification for the job of PD.

Finally, Jane is performing well today at a Radio station in the Northeast. She's nurtured and paid well. She returns the favor with great shows every day, super remotes, personal appearances and a strong personal involvement in the community through charity and civic organizations which she supports personally. In fact, management at her new station is thinking about making her PD or possibly moving her to host morning drive if either of the positions become open.

(*Editor's Note:* Legal requirements vary from state to state. Contact legal counsel in your area for specific recommendations.)

Chapter 40

Talking To Your Tekkie

By William P. Suffa

- **The most significant problem facing station and group engineering is the failure of engineers, talent and management to communicate effectively.**
- **Engineers might not understand the fundamentals of your business. But they need to understand how to "sell" their ideas using the same concepts you use to sell to advertisers.**
- **Managers should become good engineering consumers.**
- **When it comes to equipment purchases, demand data that demonstrate good value.**

I came to realize long ago that the single most significant problem facing station and group engineering is the failure of engineers, talent and management to communicate effectively.

Now you're thinking: "What does he mean, I don't communicate well with my engineers? I've done all that management training and, besides, I don't need (or want) to understand technical details." Well, I've got news for you: Your engineer doesn't understand the business details, either. In fact, your engineer might not even understand some business fundamentals. I speak from experience: I consider myself of reasonable intelligence and good educational background, but it was not until I owned my own "small" business that I truly understood some of the business aspects of broadcasting (and I still don't understand everything).

I'll use my partner's experience as an example. Along with some (mostly engineer) business partners and friends, he bought a small-market Radio station a few years ago. Together, they rebuilt the technical operation to be one of the finest around, and obtained some good programming. There was just one problem: It signed on the air, and advertisers came knocking. But guess what? That's right, no one had thought about sales. (The station later sold, for a profit, but the lesson was learned.)

It's A Deal

In the engineering/management interaction, communication comes down to a matter of sales. That is, convincing someone else that your point of view is right and making a "deal." As a manager/owner, you are the consumer when it comes to engineering matters. And your engineer should be able to "sell" you on his ideas. Usually, an engineer has the station's best interest at heart, be it better sound, greater equipment reliability, improved coverage or simply keeping the station on the air. The trouble is, most engineers don't know — or want to know — about selling. And selling is exactly what they need to do.

Let's look at three "typical" encounters:

The first encounter was related to me by a station engineer. The engineer lamented management's failure to spend money for new studio transmitter link (STL) equipment. The old equipment was so unreliable that the engineer was frequently called just to keep the station on the air. After a bit of discussion, it was obvious that the engineer had asked for the equipment without providing supporting data, and management had failed to ask the engineer to justify his request. When we demonstrated to management how a new STL could save money (in lost advertising, personnel costs and operating expense), improve the air sound and reduce downtime, the station purchased the STL in short order.

The second encounter was a situation I noticed at a medium-sized (but not rich) AM station. There were several pieces of new equipment which sat next to unused but serviceable equipment. Yet other, more critical equipment was headed for failure. In this case, management simply allowed the engineer to buy new, without ever setting a budget or evaluating the options. The engineer became complacent about maintenance and assumed that he could get new equipment anytime he wanted (even better if the old equipment "broke"). Management didn't want to know about technical things, and simply set a goal of keeping the station on the air at any cost.

Buyer Beware

In the third encounter, both the station engineer and the station owner got hoodwinked by an equipment supplier, because neither understood what they were buying. I was called in to "fix" an AM directional antenna system installed just a few years ago. The complaint: poor coverage, inability to stay on the air and poor sound. After inspecting the situation (and finding a badly designed system), we devised a new tuning system using the old parts (removing about $7,500 worth of unnecessary parts) and re-tuned the array. The "new and improved" signal and audio performance were immediately noticed by station staff and listeners. It's too soon to tell if the station will achieve greater market presence, but everyone seems impressed with the difference. As a side benefit, the maintenance costs will decrease dramatically with the simpler antenna system design. Total cost of the redesign: about $3,500.

These three examples point out the need for engineers to communicate better and for management to ask the right questions. Unlike home or car purchases, there is no textbook on what to ask. That's where a good consultant can be helpful.

I advocate an approach where the engineer becomes a good salesman, and the owner/manager becomes a good consumer. After all, you wouldn't buy a car without looking at the features and evaluating several options (including the relative costs). Consider how you sell to advertisers. Do you demonstrate the value of buying your signal and back it up with figures? Do you present several packages, or programs, representing "least expensive" and "more money but better value." These same concepts can apply to your station's technical operation.

Managers should realize that many brilliant engineers are wallflowers who can't communicate to "non-tekkies." Engineers, on the other hand, need to get out of the transmitter cabinet and understand how to sell their advice and convince managers of the need for equipment purchases or repairs (participating with the sales staff in seminars and occasional calls could do a world of good).

If you can't communicate with your engineer, or the purchase is big and complex, then it makes sense to be judicious and use a consultant with whom you feel comfortable, someone who will explain the facts of life and review equipment purchases. After all, your advertisers are buying your signal: If it's not there, or not right, the money will line your competitor's cage.

Chapter 41

Common Threads Of Success

Some Basics Will Always Be Cutting Edge

By Richard Chapin

- **Stations should be wary of "cutting edge" fads that forsake long-term focus.**
- **Radio succeeds when stations that are market-driven provide a quality, long-term sales effort for the benefit of the customer and the station.**
- **Calling on clients directly was, is and always will be "cutting-edge" sales technology.**

After 40 years of viewing the broadcasting industry from salesman to sales manager to owner/operator to broker, I have found some common threads that link the history of Radio: 1) management with focus, 2) a well-trained sales staff, 3) market-driven programming.

One of America's great football coaches, Bill Walsh, has said that while winning each game is important, winning seasons are the true measurement. Too often, the "cutting edge" is really only a passing fad. Companies quickly grab hold of the fad and lose their long-term focus. Radio succeeds when stations that are market-driven provide a quality, long-term sales effort for the benefit of the customer and the station.

The Tried And True

Today, more than ever, new "ideas" are bombarding us all the time. It is difficult to know if they have substance. To readily accept the new idea and abandon tried-and-true methods is certainly not the answer. The Radio Advertising Bureau researched and developed Instant Background in the mid-'60s, and the service is still "cutting-edge" sales technology. We are living with satellite delivery systems and talking about digital broadcast bands, but we must remember that the quality of locally driven, market-driven programming is always "cutting edge."

Recently, I had an opportunity to visit with a bright young salesperson in a sizable Southwestern market, and he made a very interesting comment. When I asked him why he was having such success with local-direct clients, this salesperson stated naively that the market had focused so long and hard on local agency business that the several hundred local-direct accounts were thrilled to see a real station representative. Calling on clients directly was, is and always will be "cutting-edge" sales technology.

We've seen it during the '80s era of junk bonds and leveraged buyouts. Investors come and go, but operators operate. Today, as it was in the '60s and '70s, Radio stations are worth what they have built through solid operations. They are judged on performance, on operating income and on their ability to maintain or increase it. Who knows what the next new gimmick will be? All of us should be ready and anxious to accept new ideas — we need them. You can't deny progress. But we need new ideas as add-ons and building blocks, not wholesale changes that disrupt, create morale problems and unemployment and, yes, sometimes destroy.

Edge Of Evolution

The great Radio stations I have watched over the years are always on the "cutting edge" and a little out of sync because they do not fall for the quick-fix changes. They evolve just as surely as we saw everybody jump on the bandwagon for 60-second commercials in the '70s, to 30 seconds in the '80s and now back to 60 in the '90s. Being "in sync" about length of commercials is immaterial. Making the commercials effective for the advertiser is always "cutting-edge" technology.

Chapter 42

Success Made Simple

Common Sense Still Makes Sense

By Jack M. Rattigan

Whenever I begin a seminar or speech, I always open with this quote: "I offer nothing more than simple facts, plain arguments and common sense." That is not a new concept. It is attributed to Thomas Paine in his pre-Revolutionary publication *Common Sense.*

Successful people have always used common sense or intuition, along with imagination, originality, creativity and vision. Shoot-from-the-hip people sometimes have a lucky streak, but their achievements are rarely long term.

Every day in Radio, we have opportunities to use common sense in routine and major decisions.

- **Set goals.**
- **A focused staff knows what you expect of them.**
- **A happy staff is a loyal staff.**
- **Courtesy sets a good example and is good for business.**
- **Investigate alternatives before making major decisions.**
- **Be a leader, not a detractor.**
- **Appreciate people who do things right — and say thank you.**

Exceptional Yet Realistic

• Do you set goals? Do you have a plan for your station and your staff, or do you and your staff just show up for work every day hoping it will be better than yesterday? It is common sense to have a plan.

• Do you keep your staff focused? Do you guide without dictating? Do you set standards that are exceptional yet realistic? Does everyone know what is expected of them? Do you regularly review your progress and areas that need improvement? It is common sense to be focused.

• Do you keep your staff happy? Is your station a happy place to work? Do you treat your staff with dignity? Do you praise in public and reprimand in private? Do you drive away good people, or do you support your people so that they are loyal and dedicated to the station? (Loyalty and longevity are essential for long-term success. Ever stop to think why we in Radio keep sending new people to see clients while the newspaper person has been calling on the same client for 20 years?) It is common sense that if you keep your staff happy, you will keep your staff.

• Do you operate an open-door policy? Can your people talk to you frankly without being afraid that anything they say can and will be used against them? Or do they know that you really care about what is on their minds and that you will accept sincere ideas and respect their opinions? It is common sense to have an open-door policy.

Gracious And Refined

• Are you courteous? Regardless of the pressures of the day, do you maintain professional and businesslike deportment? Do you keep appointments on time? Do you return phone calls promptly? Do your associates and acquaintances consider you gracious and refined? It is common sense to be courteous.

• Do you speak their language? When you are with clients, are you knowledgeable about their business and marketing situation? Do you show empathy to their problems, and are you committed to work with them as a partner in marketing rather than someone who just wants their money? It is common sense to know how to speak your clients' language.

• Do you investigate alternatives? When you are about to make a major decision or expenditure, do you consider diverse proposals? After consideration, do you make a firm decision to move on rapidly to set the plan into action? It is common sense to consider alternatives before making major decisions.

• Do you call on past experiences? Have you learned not to make the same mistakes? Do you glean something new from every event? Do you put the learning into practice? It is common sense to learn from experience.

Ample Appreciation

• Are your people up to date on the latest developments in our industry? Do you have an ongoing training program? Is it an organized agenda through a company or outside trainer? If not, do you send your people to periodic training seminars or workshops? It is common sense to continue learning.

• Do you make things happen? Is your station a front-runner in programming, marketing, creative promotions and community activities? Are you a leader in your local Radio association? Do you work with broadcast colleagues to promote Radio as an effective advertising medium, or do you trash other stations and then wonder why advertisers think Radio is a poor investment? It is common sense to be a leader, not a detractor.

• Do you show appreciation? Do you say "thank you" often enough? Do you acknowledge people who are doing something right, or do you talk to your people only when they do something you don't approve of? It is common sense to be appreciative.

There are no secret schemes or miracle blueprints here. There are a lot of questions, but you have the answers. It's just common sense.

Chapter 43

Remote Broadcasts

How Do You Get There From Here?

By Roy Pressman

Radio stations have been doing remote broadcasts for years. Every weekend, they're all over the dial, and clients love them. But there's a lot more to remote broadcasts than meets the ear, so proper planning and preparation are necessary to cut costs and increase reliability.

- **Three essentials for a remote broadcast are: 1) a way to get audio from the remote site to your studio, 2) a way to communicate with your air studio, 3) a way to listen to your station.**
- **A frequency extender can make broadcast-quality transmission possible over a regular telephone line.**
- **SW 56 circuits are high-speed data circuits that can send and receive digital audio, provided you have the proper adapters and converters.**

What Is A Remote?

Every station has its own ideas about what a remote actually is, but there is a common thread. All remotes involve broadcasting from a remote location for a certain period of time. It could be something as simple as a call-in from a local car dealership, or something as complex as a broadcast from Paris.

In the old days, all remote broadcast programming (music, commercials, promos/jingles) came from the remote site. But now we do things differently. Only the microphone audio has to feed the station from the remote site; music and commercials can be played normally from the on-air studio. This greatly reduces the possibilities of technical problems and maintains the quality of your music and commercials.

The Essentials

You need three things for any remote: 1.) a way to get audio from the remote site to your studio, 2.) a way to communicate with your air studio, 3.) a way to listen to your station.

Remotes come in all shapes and sizes, and they depend on your goal. The longer the remote, the more critical the quality — provided the music/commercials are played from the air studio. For example, if you were doing call-ins from the local car dealership, a regular telephone line or cellular telephone might be sufficient. If you need better quality, then you'll have to do some planning.

There are three ways of getting your remote-site audio back to the studio: telephone lines (there are many types), remote pickup units (RPUs) and cellular telephones. RPU systems (available from both Marti Electronics and Moseley Associates) use transmitters and receivers similar to a station's studio-to-transmitter link, but they utilize specially allocated frequencies for this purpose. The RPU system allows you to be independent of the telephone company, and you can set up the remote at a moment's notice.

RPU Systems — Pro And Con

The positives of the RPU systems include: high quality, no telephone line charges and quick setup.

The negatives of using the RPU are:

1.) RPU equipment must be purchased (transmitters/receivers/antennas/masts), and you must obtain a license from the FCC for the system. There are a limited number of RPU frequencies available, so you will have to coordinate with other stations in your area before applying for the RPU license. You might be required to share a frequency with another station in your area. There are three different types of RPU channels, with different levels of quality: 50 kHz channel (50 Hz to 10.5 kHz); 25 kHz channel (50 Hz to 7.5 kHz); 10 kHz (50 Hz to 3.0 kHz).

2.) There might be monthly tower rental fees for RPU receiver sites.

3.) RPU systems are subject to (possibly malicious) interference.

4.) Usually you must have line-of-sight from the transmit antenna to the RPU receive antenna.

5.) You might need multiple receiver sites to cover your entire service area.

Lines Vs. Loops

There are two types of telephone lines: "POT" (plain old telephone lines), like the kind you have at home, and equalized telephone loops or circuits. The equalized circuits are available in three configurations: 5 kHz, 8 kHz and 15 kHz. The number refers to the upper-frequency response limit of the line. A regular telephone line has a frequency response of 300-3 kHz. (No highs and no lows!) The equalized circuits usually have very good low-frequency response but have limited upper-frequency response. Don't get lost in all these numbers and letters; the real question is, what circuit does each individual application need? A 5 kHz circuit should be OK for most AM voice-only remotes but will be noticeably dull on an FM station. An 8 kHz circuit will be sufficient for voice/music for AM and voice-only on FM. The 15 kHz circuit is only necessary for remotes requiring stereo music broadcast from the remote site (you will need two circuits for stereo). Please refer to the application chart below:

REMOTE BROADCAST TRANSMISSION INFORMATION

REMOTE TYPE	FREQUENCY RESPONSE:	VOICE APPLICATIONS:		MUSIC APPLICATIONS:		COSTS:	
		AM	FM	AM	FM	Line	Equipment
1. Regular Telephone Line	300 - 3 kHz	poor	marginal	unacceptable	unacceptable	$	$
2. Single-Line Frequency Extender	50 - 3 kHz	fair	poor	unacceptable	unacceptable	$	$$
3. Two-Line Frequency Extender	50 - 5 kHz	good	fair	Fair	unacceptable	$$	$$$
4. Three-Line Frequency Extender	50 - 8 kHz	excellent	good	good	fair	$$$	$$$$$
5. Equalized Telephone Line 5 kHz	50 - 5 kHz	excellent	fair	fair	unacceptable	$$$	$
6. Equalized Telephone Line 8 kHz	50 - 8 kHz	excellent	good	good	fair	$$$$	$
7. Equalized Telephone Line	15 kHz	excellent	excellent	excellent	excellent	$$$$$	$
8. Switch 56 Digital Circuit	50 - 7.5 kHz	excellent	good	excellent	fair	$$$$$	$$$$$
9. Dual Switch 56 Digital Circuit	50 - 15 kHz	excellent	excellent	excellent	excellent	$$$$$$$	$$$$$$$$
10. Remote Pickup 10 kHz Channel	50 - 3 kHz	fair	poor	unacceptable	unacceptable	0	$$$$$$
11. Remote Pickup 25 kHz Channel	50 - 7.5 kHz	excellent	good	excellent	fair	0	$$$$$$$
12. Remote Pickup 50 kHz Channel	50 - 10.5 kHz	excellent	excellent	excellent	good	0	$$$$$$$$

The Magical Frequency Extender

How do you improve the quality and frequency response of a regular telephone line? Use a frequency extender. These devices trick the phone line and make broadcast-quality transmission over regular phone lines a reality. Regular telephone lines are usually available and cost much less to install and maintain. Frequency extenders come in single-line, two-line and three-line units. Comrex and Gentner have numerous products on the market. If you want all your eggs in one basket, look into a product by Cellcast that combines a cellular phone, mixer, timer and frequency extender all in one package.

Switch 56: Digital Data

In many areas of the country, there is a new service available called Switch 56. Each telephone company has its own name for the service; Southern Bell calls it Accupulse. The SW 56 circuits are actually high-speed data circuits that can send and receive digital audio, provided you have the proper adapters and converters. The adapters, called data service units (DSUs), are similar to a typical computer modem; the converters, called coder/decoders or digital audio codecs, convert analog to digital and digital to analog.

Each circuit provides bidirectional 50-7.5 kHz frequency response with no audible noise or distortion. If you utilize two SW 56 circuits and the proper codecs/DSUs, you can get stereo/50-15 kHz circuits. Because this technology is new, installation charges can be expensive. This may discourage you from utilizing this service for local one-time remote broadcasts. Check with Comrex and CCS for more information on Switch 56.

Dealing With Ma Bell

Call your telephone company at least one month before your broadcast to order telephone lines or circuits. Have the circuit(s)/lines installed one week before the broadcast and specify that they be disconnected one week after the broadcast. There will usually be a charge for installation and one-month minimum usage. If there is no access to a regular telephone at the remote site, you might order a regular telephone line for communications as well. Installation charges can run from several hundred to several thousand dollars, depending on the circuit and your telephone company.

What's Your Line?

There are two ways to send your remote broadcast back to the studio: via wire or via Radio (RPU). Talk with your engineer and find out how congested your area's RPU frequencies are. Take a look at your capital budget: Are you willing to commit a large amount of cash to build an RPU system to cover your service area? Check with the telephone company on installation charges for the various types of telephone lines. How many remotes are you going to do this year, and how important is the quality? Talk with your equipment dealer to find out exact equipment costs for the systems that we have reviewed. With this information, you will be able to decide which remote systems are right for you.

Chapter 44

Use Factoring To Increase Cash Flow

One Of The Oldest Forms Of Financing

By Cliff Boyd

The federal government is keeping a close watch over financial institutions today, so banks have become even more cautious about their commercial lending practices. This situation has caused severe problems in the business community.

Traditionally, banks have used four basic forms of financing: line of credit, term loan, inventory loan and the accounts receivable loan. Stations that have depended on these traditional financing methods recently have been put in an unstable position, with their funding reduced and, in some cases, banks calling their loans. Consequently, many stations are being forced to seek alternative financing sources. One option is to use factoring.

A Prominent Vehicle

A factor is a company that provides businesses with operating capital by purchasing their accounts receivable. Factoring, one of the oldest forms of financing, has become the most prominent vehicle for providing operating capital to businesses in the '90s. However,

- **In today's cautious lending environment, businesses are seeking alternative forms of financing, such as factoring.**
- **A factor is a company that provides businesses with operating capital by purchasing their accounts receivable.**
- **Commercial factoring works the same way as consumer factoring, which takes place when a credit card is used to make a purchase.**
- **The No. 1 reason a company uses a factor is because of accelerated growth.**
- **Unlike a bank that is depending on the creditworthiness of the customer, a factor is concerned with the creditworthiness of its customer's debtors.**
- **A factor should meet some basic requirements, including: service, ability to grow and stability.**

most people do not fully understand it.

Factoring reaches virtually every segment of the business community. Any company that sells a product or provides a service to another company could be a candidate for factoring. What many people (even those in financial circles) don't realize is that factoring is used more than all other types of financing combined. Whenever an individual or company uses a credit card, a factoring transaction takes place. This is consumer factoring, but it works exactly the same way as commercial factoring.

When a credit card is used to purchase a product or service, the merchant or business accepts a credit slip as payment. The slips are then sent to the credit card company or bank. The business then receives cash before the credit card holder pays the bill. If a business had to wait until the customer paid the credit card bill, it would have a severe cash flow problem. By receiving the immediate cash, a business doesn't tie up all of its working capital in accounts receivable. In order to receive immediate cash for the credit card slips and to provide customers with credit terms, the business is willing to pay a discount. Typically a business will pay a 2 percent to 4 percent discount fee. This means that for every $100 in credit card slips submitted to the financial institution, the business will receive $96 to $98 in immediate cash. Commercial factoring accomplishes the same for wholesale businesses. It releases the cash tied up in accounts receivable and gives a company the working capital it needs.

Some companies try to increase cash flow by offering a discount for prompt payment. Typically a 2 percent net 10 days discount is common. The problem with this kind of incentive is that the customer may not pay in 10 days but still will take the discount. The other problem is the company still doesn't have the immediate cash flow.

Growth Creates Need

It is true that factoring is not for every company. A typical company that uses a factor may fall into one of several categories, but the No. 1 reason a company uses a factor is because of accelerated growth. With increased sales and growth come increased expenses and more accounts receivable. By releasing the money tied up in accounts receivable, a company can increase the cash flow it needs to expand.

Approval Process Is Key

The first question most people ask about factoring is: How can a factor provide financing when a bank will not? The answer to the question, and the key to factoring, is the approach and approval process. Unlike a bank that is depending on the creditworthiness of the customer, a factor is concerned with the creditworthiness of its customer's debtors.

Traditionally, a bank is going to want security equal to at least three times the amount of additional working capital provided by factoring.

There are many things that factoring does for a company. It can improve a company's cash position. Along with the additional working capital comes the ability to increase production and generate more sales. There is something else factoring can do that is not readily apparent: It can improve a company's credit rating. When a company has cash flow, it can pay its bills, increase inventory and equipment purchases and maintain a greater daily balance in the company checking account.

Selecting A Factor

Choosing a factor is like selecting any other professional service. The fees, services and reputation can vary dramatically from factor to factor. It is important to find a factor that can provide your company with the help it needs. There is specific information you should have about a factor before you make a selection:

1.) Make sure the factor will provide you with all the services that have been discussed in this chapter.

2.) It is important for the factor to have the financial strength to service your needs as you grow. Ask if the company is backed by a major financial institution. Many factors are totally dependent on investment capital. With this type of financial arrangement, money may not be available when a company needs it.

3.) Many factors come into the marketplace only to go out of business. A factor should have experience and stability in the marketplace. A good indicator is a factor that has been in business over 10 years.

4.) A factor that has offices nationwide is better able to service a client's account.

5.) The funding capabilities of a factor are important. If a factor has the ability to grow with a company, it should be able to fund up to $2 million a month.

6.) You should never be asked to pay an application or processing fee. The company should provide a complete proposal with all terms spelled out at no cost.

7.) A factor with a variety of services is better able to provide a company with a proposal that will meet specific needs.

In the coming years, factoring will continue to play an important part in providing the business community with an alternative form of financing.

Chapter 45

Pest Control

Beware The Creature Invasion

By Rick Ott

Chances are that one or more of these cunning creatures is inhabiting your station. See if you recognize any as we discuss their characteristics.

- **Crazed Complicators strive to create an illusion of indispensability by making their jobs seem incredibly complex.**
- **Bytemites lose sight of the human element, and focus instead on the amount of data they can grind out of their computers.**
- **Effort Evaders often expend great effort attempting to avoid effort.**
- **Problem Creators feel compelled to keep a steady stream of problems coming to maintain their self-image as disaster-saver.**
- **Ostriches never recognize a problem, even when they're drowning in one.**

Confusion & Illusion

• *The Crazed Complicator*. Some people believe their particular job is a Byzantine and convoluted endeavor. Or at least they try to make others think so. Crazed Complicators strive to create an illusion of power and indispensability by making things seem incredibly complex, and making themselves look like the only ones capable of handling the "enormity" of it all.

The two primary traits of the Crazed Complicator are a heavy reliance on paperwork (their work stations are often brimming with reports and printouts) and/or colorful rhetoric. You know you're dealing with a Crazed Complicator when you ask a simple question and get five minutes of a nebulous, undefinable answer. Or, if they do come up with a definitive, understandable answer, you can ask them the same question the next day and get a completely different answer.

Real value is created by simplifying — making things easier to understand and use by others. But Crazed Complicators do the opposite, believing it's in their best interest. Interestingly, Crazed Complicators can rise to positions of prominence, depending on their own finesse and the susceptibility of those they snow.

• *The Bytemite.* If you're in Radio, you're in the entertainment business. Specifically, you're in the business of stimulating emotions, which is the real function of entertainment. But Bytemites lose sight of the human, emotional element, believing instead that success is based on the amount of data they can grind out of their computers.

The primary characteristic of the Bytemite is the inordinate amount of time spent in front of the CRT screen. They're most often found in the research and programming areas. In the past decade, many program directors have evolved into first-rate Bytemites, having been seduced by their computerized music rotation systems. When a candidate for a PD position brags about computer skills instead of knowledge of human behavior, you're dealing with a classic Bytemite.

(On the other hand, computers play a justifiably major role in traffic and accounting. People in those departments who spend a good amount of time at the computer are doing what they're supposed to be doing, and shouldn't be confused with the Bytemite.)

Amazing Avoidance

• *The Effort Evader.* The Effort Evader believes that exerting any effort above the absolute minimum is too supreme a sacrifice. They're constantly looking for shortcuts and patchwork solutions. They perform one small notch above what would get them fired, but no more.

Instead, the Effort Evader believes that others are dutifully bound to exert any effort necessary to "make my job easier." Yet they never do anything that makes someone else's job easier, nor do they work one minute of overtime without complaining.

Ironically, Effort Evaders often expend great effort attempting to avoid effort. They put a lot of thought, creativity and time into maneuvering themselves into positions that ride others' coattails. Effort Evaders don't realize that if they concentrated as much on productive endeavor, they'd be 10 times more valuable — and would get 10 times the reward.

• *The Problem Creator.* Every station has one self-appointed individual who assumes this position. He or she believes that their own stock rises in direct proportion to the number of problems they can spot.

The Problem Creator not only scrutinizes everything for hidden problems (including things outside their area of responsibility), but even projects problem scenarios where none actually exist. Problem Creators feel compelled to keep a steady stream of problems coming to maintain their self-image as station disaster-saver.

Problem Creators are easy to spot in meetings. They love to shoot holes through every idea or proposal that comes up for discussion. But they seldom offer solutions and seldom work to prevent problems, since doing each would negate their problem prophesies.

Heads In The Sand

• *The Ostrich.* As the extreme opposite of the Problem Creator, the Ostriches never recognize a problem, even when they're drowning in one. Interestingly, the Ostrich is often found in management rather than in the lower ranks.

The Ostriches subconsciously believe that acknowledging problems is admitting weakness in themselves as a manager. Consequently, they either angrily blame others for things that go wrong or allow things to deteriorate past the point of practical correction. The Ostrich sabotages his or her own success by failing to acknowledge, face and correct problems as they appear.

Each of these creatures exists because someone in the organization is reinforcing their behavior. Are you inadvertently rewarding people (with compliments, raises, promotions, etc.) for handling "complex" situations, "mastering" computer systems to the neglect of other responsibilities, putting forth less effort than they are cable of, squawking whenever they spot a potential problem and ignoring real problems? Believe it or not, many managers do reward this kind of behavior. If you have any of these creatures inhabiting your station, it's time to assess your own behavior and make adjustments.

Chapter 46

Inspection Protection

Be Prepared For A Visit From The FCC

By Roy Pressman

When deregulation became reality, it seemed as if the FCC was finally going to let broadcasters self-regulate the broadcast business. Many requirements were changed and/or eliminated, but the burden of how to stay legal became the broadcaster's responsibility. The FCC demonstrated that it would come down hard on violators of the remaining regulations.

- **Use an inspection checklist to prepare for FCC inspections.**
- **Certain documents must be posted in your air studio. A three-ring binder is a handy way to mount them on the wall.**
- **All on-air personalities must have a Restricted Radiotelephone Operator's Permit or other commercial Radio license that does not preclude operation of a broadcast facility.**
- **A Station Technical Procedure Manual should be on hand in your studio. Make sure the air staff is familiar with it.**

Inspection Checklist

First step: Obtain one of the many FCC inspection checklists that are available, such as the NAB's Radio Broadcaster's Inspection Checklist (L-9304) or the checklist available from the FCC field offices. Go through the checklist with your engineer and focus on areas that could leave you open for infractions/large fines. The FCC wants you to be prepared for an inspection, so its checklist details exactly what it will ask for when and if it visits you. Take some time and do your homework.

Studio Stroll

Let's take a quick walk through your station's air studio and look at a few areas that can help prevent an expensive FCC fine.

Certain documents must be posted in the air studio (or control point).

These documents don't have to be framed but must be kept in an accessible and visible area in the studio. A neat idea is to remove the front and back cover from a loose-leaf binder, leaving the three-ring binder assembly. Attach the assembly to a piece of wood with some screws and mount the wood/binder in the air studio. Place all necessary documents in clear plastic sleeves and put them in the binder.

Here's what to look for:

1.) Your station license

2.) Construction permits (if any)

3.) Renewals (usually in postcard form)

4.) STAs (Special Temporary Authority)

5.) Auxiliary transmitter/antenna licenses

6.) All transmitter operator's licenses. All of your on-air personalities must have licenses posted in your air studio, without exception. When new personalities are hired, make sure they have a valid license (Restricted Radiotelephone Operator's Permit or other commercial Radio license that does not preclude operation of a broadcast facility). Obtain several FCC Form 753s from your local field office. Require operators without a license to fill out, sign and mail the form to the FCC. Once this form is properly filled out, an operator is allowed to temporarily operate a broadcast station until receiving a permanent license from the FCC. (The current fee for the Restricted Radiotelephone Operator's Permit is $35.)

7.) Written designation of chief operator: It wasn't long ago when stations were required to have a chief engineer or contract engineer with an FCC First Class license. This requirement was replaced with the chief operator designation. The chief operator must hold at least a restricted Radiotelephone Operator's license. He or she essentially performs the duties of the chief engineer without the requirement of holding a First Class/General Class Commercial license.

The "designation of chief operator" is nothing more than a short statement signed by the station general manager that names a particular person as the chief operator of your station. It must be posted in the air studio. If you are using a contract engineer, a written contract should be available on request by FCC personnel.

Write It Down

8.) Transmitter log: Although you are not required to take transmitter readings every three hours, you must ensure that your station is within legal power limits. Require your on-air people to log transmitter readings every three hours. Have your engineer/chief operator post a chart identifying legal transmitter parameters. The chief operator should review and sign the transmitter logs on a daily basis.

Required log entries:

• Adjustment of any technical operating parameters and further description if adjustment was to correct an out-of-tolerance situation. Description of any repairs to transmitter system or antenna.

• Tower light repairs/replacements. (Make sure the time and date are logged.) Although the FCC no longer requires this, check your tower lights at least once every 24 hours, preferably in the evening.

• Date and time of each EBS test that is sent or received. You might also be required to log additional information. Check your station license for any special conditions required by the FCC.

9.) EBS Checklist And Authenticator Word List: Check the date on your EBS Checklist. If you need to update your EBS materials, contact the FCC at (202) 632-3906. Post all EBS materials in a clearly marked folder next to your license binder.

10.) Station Technical Procedure Manual: Although not required, there should be a reference manual in the studio containing the following topics:

a. How to take transmitter readings.

b. How to turn the transmitter on and off.

c. How to raise and lower the power.

d. How to determine if the station's power output is within legal limits. (There should be an accompanying chart.)

e. What to do if the station is not within legal power limits.

f. Emergency procedures: How to change over to your backup transmitter (provided you have one).

g. How to transmit an EBS test.

h. How to log EBS tests (both received and transmitted).

i. Telephone number list, including all main and standby engineers, general manager and program director.

j. What to do if the tower lights malfunction.

Set up a meeting with your air staff and review all materials in your Technical Procedure Manual. The FCC requires you to make sure that your on-air staff is familiar with all technical operational procedures, so it's wise to thoroughly go over all materials contained in your manual.

Just Be Prepared

Be prepared for an inspection. Obtain an inspection checklist and set up a mock inspection at your facility. Discuss all applicable FCC rules and regulations with your engineer and legal counsel. Don't procrastinate; fix problem areas immediately. You can protect yourself from violations that could result in steep fines.

Chapter 47

Management Can't Motivate

But You Can Activate

By Dave Gifford

- **Motivation comes from within the individual.**
- **Either you have a driving, inner urge to succeed or you don't.**
- **Management can change behavior, not attitudes.**
- **You have to hire attitudes.**
- **Management can activate, not motivate.**

Was David Koresh a great motivator? If being a great motivator is getting people to do what you want them to do willingly, primarily because of your influence, then David Koresh was a great motivator. By that standard alone, then so too were Adolf Hitler, Ghandi, Dr. Martin Luther King Jr., Helen of Troy, Joan of Arc, Queen Victoria, Golda Meir and, in the present tense, Lee Iacocca, Mother Teresa and Madonna. Think about it.

In my opinion, none of those people ever motivated anyone. Why?

The argument as to whether a given individual can or cannot motivate another individual is still in dispute today, even among the experts.

The Gurus Argue

On the yes-you-can-motivate side of the argument are the likes of Warren Bennis and Peter Drucker. Bennis, best known for his watershed books on leadership, years ago defined motivation as communicating a vision that others can believe in and then helping them convert that vision into organizational gains. Drucker, the guru of management gurus, counsels his clients to motivate by managing by objectives, by building teams to achieve those objectives and by encouraging communication at all levels.

Equally impressive, however, is the lineup of nay-sayers that includes behavioral scientist Abraham Maslo, clinical psychologist Frederick Herzberg and social scientist Douglas McGregor. All three argue that motivation comes from within the individual and that motivation in the workplace cannot be achieved without first satisfying an individual's higher personal needs.

Then there is John Adair, the brilliant English scholar who contends (his "50-50 Rule," a modification of Pareto's 80-20 principle) that motivation is equally divided between an individual's self-motivation and other external forces such as leadership.

So, who am I to get in the middle of an argument in this company, right? Well, for the sake of your amusement, if not enlightenment, let me give it a shot, beginning with the fact that the dictionary defines "motivate" as "to provide with a motive." As a practicing student as well as teacher of management, my personal life experiences over 36 years in this business have taught me what follows:

In every management-employee communication, there is a sender and a receiver. Given that the hired-fired laws of leverage in a Radio station are all written by management, management's role is mostly that of the sender, with the employee usually ending up the receiver. My problem with the yes-you-can argument is that it is sender-based only, with no consideration whatsoever for the possible unwillingness of the receiver to be motivated by anyone.

Some managers do have a vision and, because they possess a certain charisma, plus the skills of persuasion and the cheerleading, team-building magic it takes to activate a sales staff, they are indeed able to translate that vision into measurable results. Key word: "activate," not motivate. But, what happens when the vision sent is not the vision received? Just as not every manager can motivate (conventional definition), it is true that not every employee can be motivated.

Leading The Self-Motivated

How well do you think Lee Iacocca's (alleged) motivational powers might have served him had his key employees been unmotivated rather than self-motivated? Then Mr. Iacocca might confess that his reputation as a great motivator came about only after he shook up the Chrysler Corp. and began to surround himself with key self-motivated employees.

If a great motivator must have a certain command of the gifts and tools of influence to motivate employees, then the people they are supposed to motivate must also possess certain inner qualities to be motivated.

For example, if you were to analyze only those successful salespeople you managed over the years, chances are you'd discover a commonalty: They all had a success-driven orientation to begin with. Either they were all willing to pay the price of success or they all had a certain competitive resolve, or both. And, because of their own self-confidence, personal pride, commitment to improve themselves, need for recognition and self-actualization and/or because of their own sense of personal greed, over time they developed an ability to communicate in such a way that their desire or compulsion to persuade was satisfied. They became successful only because, as self-motivated individuals with a driving inner urge to succeed, they just couldn't help but succeed. In other words, they became successful not because of you, however damaging that may be to your ego, but because of themselves.

But, you may argue, there were many times when their performance improved only because of your input, and you are probably 100 percent correct. However, to suggest that you have the ability to motivate someone is to suggest that you have the ability to change attitudes and, as all human behaviorist scholars agree, that is impossible. Management can change behavior but not attitudes.

Re-Cocking The Motivation Trigger

What you did do, in those situations where you made a difference, was to change their behavior. You re-cocked the trigger that was already there because the motive was already there; you did not "provide the motive." In effect, because motivation cannot be internalized from an external source, you activated the mechanism of self-motivation. You didn't motivate them, you activated them.

To understand fully, it's important to recognize the difference between the popular notion of motivating someone and the act of inspiring someone, as in a seminar. Whereas I don't have the ability to motivate someone, I do have the ability to activate and inspire someone. The problem with the latter, as we all know, is that a good night's sleep can usually kill, overnight, whatever inspiration you got from a seminar the day before. The self-motivated people who decide to activate what they learned benefit the most. The difference is that they didn't come for motivation, they brought that with them … they came for "information." This proves once again that "the teacher arrives when the student is ready to learn." Attitude — that's what it's all about.

True, by threatening your employees' job security, you can get people to do what you want them to do out of fear alone, but for how long? The better option is to get them to do, willingly, what you want them to do.

It is critical that we recognize management's limitations. Management can activate, not motivate, and management can change behavior, not attitudes. You have to hire attitudes. If you hire the right people in the first place, the argument as to whether or not you can motivate someone is moot.

Now, if you think I'm wrong, I suggest that you also analyze all those salespeople who worked for you who were unsuccessful. Chances are, they all shared something in common as well. Right! Because they were not self-motivated, they couldn't be motivated.

Chapter 48

Blanketing Interference

Keeping Your Signal Where It Belongs

By William P. Suffa

"I don't give a #&%@ about those people near the tower. Just make sure we have the No. 1 signal in the market." Bad attitude. Real bad attitude. But, if you've ever owned or managed a station with a blanketing interference problem, you've likely had those thoughts. Of all the interference cases to resolve, there is almost nothing as frustrating (or contentious) as blanketing.

Blanketing interference can refer to several forms of interference that affect Radio and television reception or operation of electronic devices close to a transmitter site. The name implies that the Radio signals are so strong, they override or "blanket" everything else. Typically, blanketing interference (from a neighbor's viewpoint) will impair Radio and television reception, cause your station to be heard over telephones, intercoms and stereos, or affect the public address system of the nearby church.

- **Blanketing interference can refer to several forms of interference that affect Radio and television reception or operation of electronic devices close to a transmitter site.**
- **A rapid and competent response to interference complaints can save lots of aggravation later.**
- **Three principles to remember are: Document everything, retain technical assistance and bend over backward to assist your neighbors.**
- **Going beyond FCC requirements can buy goodwill and help the station look good if the case goes to the FCC.**

If your station should become the target of such complaints, you'll do OK if you learn these three principles and apply them: 1) document, document, document; 2) retain competent and experienced technical assistance at the outset; 3) bend over backward to assist your neighbors, even when you don't have to. If you remember these three principles, you'll minimize the chance of a long, nasty, public neighborhood (and FCC) fight.

No Wet Blankets

Blanketing interference generally doesn't result in a neighborhood problem unless you make major changes in your facility (a new site, increase in power or change in antenna height). If the application for that facility change was made in the last few years, the FCC required a certification that the station would resolve all interference affecting receivers in use prior to construction of the facility. The FCC rules require even more: The station must correct, at its expense, any blanketing complaint received during the first year following construction of the new facility. For complaints received after that period, or from locations beyond a specified distance, the station need only provide information on resolving the interference.

For administrative purposes, FM blanketing interference is defined as interference that occurs within the 115 dBu (500 mV/m) contour of the Radio station. Specifically excluded are audio devices, defective receivers, telephones, portable receivers and high gain television antennas and booster amplifiers. This is an important exclusion, especially when the complainants take their case to the FCC. For AM stations, the 1,000 mV/m contour is the blanketing contour. Exceptions for AM stations are more nebulous but follow the same principles.

If you're about to light up a new transmitter or site, consider the FCC blanketing rules to be the technical equivalent of an EOE program. Document well, and plan ahead; don't just put a wet blanket on your head and pretend the problems don't exist.

Good Neighbor Policy

The basic rule of thumb here is to keep good records and retain good technical counsel experienced in interference resolution. Bad publicity will come looking for you if you don't deal with your neighbors in a prompt and respectful manner.

The most important thing to do is to document everything. Consider this to be a legal case that will end up in court. You should designate a single staffer to follow up on interference complaints. All persons answering telephones must be trained to record on a form all the important information about the case: Name of complainant, address, devices affected, nature of the interference, date of complaint, time of call and the date and time that the complainant first noticed the interference. Then follow up. Your staff person should visit the complainant to observe the interference. The station engineer or local TV repairman should be present during the visit to observe and, if possible, fix the problem. Often, a TV filter is all that's necessary, but sometimes the TV or Radio must be replaced with a model less susceptible to interference. After the visit, indicate on the complaint form the date and time of visit and the disposition of the case. Schedule a definite time for follow-up.

File all related records for easy reference. Do not destroy any records or correspondence related to a case. Make sure you get advice of counsel (legal and engineering) early on. There have been cases where the neighbors spent big bucks to hire FCC legal and engineering counsel against the station.

The third rule is to be a good neighbor. Do you remember that the FCC has "exceptions" to the blanketing rule? Well, a few dollars spent on resolving telephone or audio problems can be worthwhile. An example: A client of ours turned on his new FM station, playing AC music. The nearby Baptist church picked up the FM signal on the speaker system used by the pastor. Since the interference fell into the FCC's excluded category, the station wanted to ignore the problem. Upon our advice, the station worked with the pastor to resolve the problem. We found out later that the church had been organizing a letter-writing campaign to their representative in Congress to try to revoke the station's construction permit. Instead, the church became an ally in helping the station resolve legitimate interference complaints in other homes nearby, and kept more than 25 complaints from ever reaching the FCC.

Chapter 49

Four Steps To Managing Anyone

Motivation And Communication Get The Job Done

By Mimi Donaldson

> - **Tell people clearly what to do.**
> - **Give them a reason to do it.**
> - **Give them the tools and resources they need to do the job.**
> - **Give feedback — positive or corrective.**

Managing means getting results through people. We do this in many different settings from workplace to household. If you are alive, you have already been a manager. You've managed delivery people, repair people, pets, children, in-laws, spouses and more.

At the station, the myth is that you need to throw money at people to motivate hard work and loyalty. Not entirely true. Management has less to do with charisma than with consistency. Managers depend on effective interpersonal communication skills to get things done.

Empower And Motivate

Many of you are called "boss." To avoid being called "boss" as a four-letter word, follow these four steps:

Step 1: Tell the person clearly what you expect them to do. Easier said than done. In management-training environments, this is called "delegation." My definition of "delegate" is to empower and motivate a person to accomplish results for which you are ultimately responsible. Delegation includes these guidelines: Choose a person capable of doing the job; explain the result you want; give the authority to get it done; monitor the activity; give recognition or praise along the way.

• Set the climate. Be sure you're in a place conducive to concentration and at a time when the person can concentrate. Listen to your words as you set the tone. Over the years, I've heard many a harried manager unwittingly say: "Now this is a simple, mindless task … that's why I'm giving it to you." Not very motivating.

• Give the big picture. Describe the overall objectives. People need to see where their part fits into the whole to feel part of the loftier goal.

• Describe steps of the task. This is the meat of the delegation discussion. Sometimes these are already printed in an instruction or procedures manual. You still need to go over these steps, however briefly, with the capable person to assure yourself of their familiarity with them. If the steps are not already written out, have the person write them out as you speak them. This increases the probability of learning them.

• Cite resources available. Point out where there are other references on the task, if any. Resources include people who have done the task or parts of it before.

• Invite questions. Even if it feels as if you don't have time to do this, it's worth it. Better to spend the time up front than be unhappily surprised later. Invite questions with open-ended prompting, such as: "What questions do you have?" not: "You don't have any questions, do you?"

• Get the person to summarize what they will do to get the job done. This takes guts on your part; you risk being answered with a defensive "Do you think I'm stupid?" Use this sentence: "Call me compulsive — I need to have you summarize how you will get this done." When you take responsibility, you reduce defensiveness in the other person.

• Agree on a date for follow-up. How soon will depend on the complexity and value of the task. You may need time and practice to develop the fine art of follow-up without hovering.

Is It On The Test?

Step 2. Give them a reason to do the task. This is the fine art of motivating. Motivating people is impossible ... they have to motivate themselves. There must be something in it for them.

Remember when you were in third grade, sitting at a little desk in class, listening to the teacher. He or she was droning on and on, boring you to sleep. Suddenly, an obnoxious kid in the back row yelled out: "Hey, teacher, is this gonna be on the test?" You were so embarrassed to hear someone actually ask that question. But you listened very carefully to the answer. If the answer was "no," your reaction was probably: Go back to sleep — not on the test. But if the teacher said "yes," you straightened up, borrowed a pencil, started taking notes — it's on the test. Ever since then, we have done only what we perceive is on our test.

To motivate people, you have to find out what's on the test. Then you have to put your priority squarely on their test.

Money Where Your Mouth Is

Step 3. Give the person the tools and resources they need to do the job. This requirement can range from a desk and pencils to training to do the job and enough time to get it done. This is the "put-your-money-where-your-mouth-is" step. Teamwork among individuals of varied backgrounds, experience and human interactive skills does not just happen. If managers want their people to be productive and happy, they must put time and effort into training themselves and their people in technical skills and communication skills.

How Am I Doing?

Step 4. Give feedback. All people, when accomplishing a task, want to know how they're doing, even your "stars."

There are two types of feedback: positive and corrective. Here are four tips for each:

Positive feedback: 1) Make it succinct, specific and sincere. 2) Stick to praise only; don't use it as an introduction to another discussion. 3) Tell them why their accomplishment is important to you and others. 4) Don't be surprised if the person is embarrassed or suspicious. This just means they're not used to praise and need more of it.

Corrective feedback: 1) Never attack the person; attack the problem, whether it's job performance such as inaccuracy or a work habit such as lateness. 2) Keep calm. It's a problem-solving mode you're after. 3) Be prepared to tell the consequences if the problem continues — and be prepared to carry them out. 4) Don't be surprised if the person reacts with hostility. Even if you're being calm and objective, some people tend to take this discussion personally.

It takes practice and, quite often, some training and acquiring of new skills, to carry out these four steps to managing. But stick with it, because managing people, empowering them to accomplish things, makes a difference in their lives ... and yours.

Chapter 50

Power Steering

What Makes Your Boss Tick?

By Dr. Philip J. LeNoble

- **The four types of management styles are: autocratic, custodial, participative and collegial.**
- **Each management style thrives on a different source of power or a combination of sources: coercive, reward, legitimate, expert and referent.**
- **The autocratic/coercive manager does not work well in today's highly educated business environment.**
- **The collegial manager, who develops a teamwork consciousness, may be the brand of leadership of the '90s.**

You have been in the broadcast business five weeks. The person who hired you was fired after eight months, and the new sales manager has promised to change the organization from a lackluster, non-competitive station to a full-steam-ahead, cutting-edge, 21st century company. Several of your sales colleagues as well as the sales support staff are nervous about the transformation.

Will you be able to deal with the incoming new style of management? Can you recognize the sources of power that each style of manager uses? In this era of frequent job turnover, the need to harmonize with your manager's style has become increasingly time critical. A preview of these styles can help you predict behavior, as well as understand how to "manage up." If you know your manager, you can manage his or her behavior.

Power, as a means of energy, affects almost every human interaction in business, personal relationships and politics. As a manifestation of management, power can be broken down into five categories and harmonized with four basic styles of management: autocratic, custodial, participative and collegial. Each thrives on a different source of power or a combination of those sources.

Autocratic Manager/Coercive Power

The autocratic manager is totally focused on obedience. This old-fashioned style harkens back to the Industrial Revolution, when fewer managers had education or studied organizational communication. In those early days, most workers did not have the benefit of a college education and may have needed more discipline and structure. The power source of this management style is coercive — the power to make life painful through control and intimidation.

The Custodial Manager

The custodial style uses reward power by controlling job security, benefits, bonuses, retirement and health management programs. The major source of power for this management type is legitimate power, which is associated with titled positions such as president or general manager. Legitimate power is official power, carried out by controlling resources, rewarding or punishing.

The Participative And Collegial Manager

The participative and collegial styles of management are usually associated with the expert and the referent sources of power. The participative manager encourages employee participation in the corporate vision, budgeting and planning processes. Expert power arises from skills or knowledge attained through specialized learning, such as what a salesperson might gain in the field. Referent power arises from personal magnetism, charm, charisma and a belief in accomplishing objectives.

Most sources of power come in pairs. A sales manager or general manager has both legitimate power, which comes with the position, and coercive power, when they have to terminate an unproductive employee. On the other hand, these managers can combine legitimate power with reward power when they promote an employee.

Both referent power and expert power seem to operate best in participative and collegial management styles. The participative manager is more like a consultant who operates in a democratic environment, encouraging constant feedback. The participative manager is leadership-oriented and provides support to the staff.

The collegial manager, not a new management term, is considered the new brand of leadership of the '90s. This type of manager looks upon the account executives as the basis for their own successes. This style of management creates responsible behavior, develops a teamwork consciousness and gives rise to enthusiasm within the department.

Knowing how your manager ticks and understanding the forces of human behavior at work is the best way to manage up as well as down. Managing with a fast-paced organization will never be easy, but pairing management styles with the focus of power can help make sense out of what seems like madness.

Chapter 51

AM Parameters

And How To Keep The FCC Happy

By William P. Suffa

- **Routine antenna maintenance can help avoid FCC problems.**
- **Experienced and qualified personnel should make antenna adjustments.**
- **Modern equipment and designs can minimize maintenance and improve station sound.**
- **All AM owners should review and comment to the FCC on the proposal to reduce proof-of-performance requirements.**

In Chapter 46, Roy Pressman discussed FCC inspections. As a former FCC inspector, I can tell you that his piece provided some good advice about keeping the transmitting plant in order. I'd like to go into a bit of detail about keeping AM antenna systems legal.

AM directional antennas are the most cash- and labor-intensive of any in the broadcasting service, with the possible exception of shortwave stations. Because of their complexity, it is tempting to forgo capital improvements and operating expenditures that are necessary to conform with FCC requirements. As many owners and managers have found out the hard way, however, the FCC is now focusing on the operation of AM directional antennas — and the bills for their ignorance are finally coming due.

A Fine Mess

Here's the deal: Each AM directional station has six separate technical parameters that must be maintained within the limits specified in the station's FCC license. Those parameters are: common point current, common point impedence, base current ratios, antenna monitor current ratios, antenna monitor phase readings and field monitor point measurements. The first two parameters are used to compute the operating power of the station; the rest determine whether the antenna pattern shape is "legal." If any of these parameters is outside the allowed tolerances, the station is a candidate for a hefty FCC fine.

Most FCC inspectors will not accept the excuse of "it just went out of tolerance" when they uncover a violation. Thus, stations should practice routine maintenance and keep a written maintenance log, signed by the chief engineer, that demonstrates a history of compliance with the rules. Remember that the FCC defines a "willful violation" as "a failure to take adequate steps to prevent the violation from occurring."

At the minimum, an AM operator should ensure on a daily basis that the antenna monitor parameters are within FCC tolerance, on a weekly basis that the base current ratios are within FCC tolerance, on a monthly basis that the monitor point limits are below the licensed limitations and on an annual basis (or after a series of antenna tuning adjustments) that the common point resistance is correct. If any of these parameters is "out," then the antenna system must be "trimmed" to bring all the parameters back into tolerance.

This is not a job for the meek of heart or the inexperienced. If there is any doubt about the ability of the local engineer to do the work, get someone qualified to help. After all, would you trust your Acura repairs to the local car wash attendant?

If the antenna system cannot be restored to tolerance, it's time to call in a consultant experienced in array adjustment. The cost depends on the work needed and the time involved — but will probably be less than fighting a protracted legal battle at the FCC.

Exciting Prospects

There are some exciting prospects on the horizon for AM, including in-band digital transmission. Remember, though, that these developments will still require a legal, properly functioning antenna system that has adequate bandwidth performance. With the "new" AM allocation rules and improvements in technology, it might be just the time to consider an antenna system improvement project.

Many of the AM directional antennas in use today were installed more than 10 years ago. The antenna designs and installations were based on hand calculations or "cookie cutter" designs without benefit of computer optimization. Today, the best consultants and station engineers are using computer modeling techniques to reduce the burden associated with the design and tune-up of AM directional antennas. Modern equipment and antenna designs can reduce the required maintenance of an AM antenna system while improving on-the-air sound and signal strength.

Chapter 52

Sales Meeting Or Torture?

Clear Goals Make Meetings More Productive

By Gina Gallagher

- **Establish your outcome or goals for each meeting.**
- **Set criteria for measuring the meeting's success.**
- **Gain agreement on outcome of meeting.**
- **Summarize each major decision.**
- **Set up next steps/time lines.**

Does your staff ever complain about having too many meetings? Some salespeople consider sales meetings a waste of time. Whether or not this is true is irrelevant; perception and reality become the same, according to neuro-linguistic programming theory: The meaning of communication is the response you get. If you are not getting the response you want, change what you are doing.

Your weekly sales meeting is your primary group communication vehicle. To get the most out of this time, you must establish your desired outcome for each meeting. Communication without a desired outcome is like traveling without a destination.

Outcomes are the goals that have been clarified and finely honed by the use of the following five steps: aiming for a specific result; being positive; dovetailing your desires with those attending the meeting; seeing, hearing, feeling (sensory data); and entertaining short- and long-term objectives. The following can serve as a guide for conducting a successful sales meeting.

State The Outcome

Your outcome must be stated in positive terms. The outcome sets boundaries for all discussions and keeps everyone focused. Write the goal of the meeting on a flip chart. Example: This meeting is to discuss the Baby Expo structure for 1994. We will be establishing the sales criteria for all of the new packages we will be constructing.

Set Criteria For Measuring Success

The criteria — such as developing a group budget, developing individual budgets, determining the number of daily calls and closes to achieve the proposed budget, determining the top 10 targets for each salesperson and utilizing the group for brainstorming packages and refinements — should be added to the flip chart and will serve as a guide to tell the group if the outcome of the meeting has been successful.

Gain Agreement On Meeting Outcome

Check with each person to see if they agree on the stated outcomes. Once you gain agreement, you can keep the meeting focused toward the intended direction and all other issues can be dismissed as irrelevant to the meeting's purpose.

If you notice a person's mouth saying "yes" in establishing an outcome, but her head is shaking "no," decide whether to confront the incongruity right away or to wait until after the meeting. You could say: "You seem to have some reservations about accepting this outcome. Did you have something else in mind?"

Utilize The Relevancy Challenge

Remain objective. Never challenge the person, only the information. Maintain rapport with a clear and calm tone of voice. Ask how her information is relevant to your outcome. If you determine that she might have a hidden agenda, your strategy should be to make the agenda irrelevant to the outcome. Or you might discover that the outcome is relevant and add the information to the meeting. If the information is challenged after agreement on the outcome has been confirmed, the group will serve to keep each other focused.

Summarize

By summarizing each major decision, the group knows where it is and where it has been and can compare this to the planned outcome of the meeting. Summarizing serves to bind the group into agreement.

Go over these areas: achievement of meeting outcome, summarize the meeting again, major decisions, the final outcome, the next step for the group, the next step for the individuals, assign time lines for completion of next steps.

A successful meeting needs balance between structure and freedom of expression to promote creativity. You might want to budget time for playing with options. Be flexible. Use humor to keep your meetings focused and make them fun. Consider utilizing members of the sales staff to facilitate some sales meetings. By providing them with a format that has a focused outcome, you not only will have productive meetings, you will also increase the sales staff's management potential.

Chapter 53

Choose Your Mood

Beware The Mind Binders

By Dr. Sharon Crain

- **Flexibility and resiliency are essential to the mind-set of women in sales.**
- **"Response-ability" requires an awareness of the thinking patterns that determine emotions and resulting mood.**
- **Avoid becoming trapped by shoulds. Resist seeing things in either black or white.**
- **Don't believe you're a mind reader; monitor your assumptions about what others are thinking. Avoid personalizing the negative reactions of others.**

Who hasn't experienced the roller coaster ride that is part of being in sales? One day we're flying high; the next day, when our buyer has a change of heart, we can quickly plummet to the depths.

This decade promises to one of shakeouts, where rapid changes in the industry will require flexibility and resiliency. For women in sales, the ability to bounce back after disappointments will be an essential mind-set.

We now have a new understanding of the word "response-ability" — the ability to choose our response in any given situation. The secret to developing response-ability is to become aware of our thinking patterns. These patterns determine our emotions and our resulting mood.

Destructive thinking patterns called Mind Binders restrict our outlook and reduce our ability to see positive options. Let's take a brief look at some common Mind Binders.

The Tyranny Of Shoulds

This irrational thinking pattern traps us into believing people should behave and events should occur according to our desires. For example, our clients shouldn't keep us waiting so long, we should be given better accounts, we should be given more latitude to negotiate. We forget that our should is our value — not necessarily the value of others.

If you engage in polarized thinking, you see everything as either black or white. Perfectionists are especially susceptible to this tendency: If something is less than perfect, it is nothing short of a disaster. This pattern is especially destructive to a woman's sense of self-worth. If your only options are to be perfect or unacceptable, then you will be displeased with yourself most of the time, since things are seldom perfect.

Mind Reading

Mind reading is the belief that we know what other people are thinking. For example, think about the times you prepare a proposal for a client group and, upon entering the office, observe that the group is in a less than jovial mood. You gear up mentally for objections to your recommendations. Your mind-set affects your whole approach to the presentation. Rather than being enthusiastic and confident, you become guarded and defensive. As the result, you give a less-persuasive proposal.

I'm not suggesting that we ignore non-verbal cues in our environment, but we can monitor the assumptions that we make based on these cues. This allows us to choose the response that will allow us to achieve our goals.

Personalization

This distorted thinking pattern triggers the belief that we personally cause the negative reactions of others. In effect, this is a fundamentally egocentric view of the world. We unconsciously assume we have such an effect on others that we cause their emotions. If a client scowls during a presentation and asks: "Where did you get these figures?" it is easy to personalize and become defensive. Yet the client's motive for the question may have nothing to do with us.

Since our emotions and our ensuing mood follow our thoughts, the first clue to be "response-able" is to become aware of Mind Binder thinking. When we consciously direct our thinking to empowering patterns, we then have the power to be flexible and resilient — the cornerstone of our future success.

Chapter 54

Assess Duopoly Traffic Operations

Not All Systems Are Designed For Combo Job

By Bunny Hofberg

Duopoly operations provide broadcasters with the single greatest means of increasing salable rating shares and sending market revenues to new heights. With a number of sales pending approval and closure, it is time that broadcasters carefully examine and calculate the total operational effect of how their stations will run.

The right traffic and accounting system for your duopoly operation depends greatly on the overall operational goal. Various scenarios are being played out in the industry. Here are a few examples:

- **Not all traffic systems have been designed to effectively and efficiently handle more than one or two stations.**
- **Define the specific needs of the duopoly operation.**
- **Contact the different software vendors, even systems that you are not currently using.**
- **Find out how long the software vendor has been providing duopoly software.**

A Whole New System

Scenario I. You own an AM/FM and acquire a second AM/FM operation within the same market. Each AM/FM operation has its own traffic and accounting system, supplied by two separate vendors.

Your overall goal is to consolidate the operations under one roof, combining the sales departments into one unit with the ability to sell the stations in combo or separately. You present specific requirements:

1.) Single traffic order capability for multiple station buys.

2.) Multiple station buy orders entered on one screen.

3.) Single database of all stations, with the ability to track each station's billing separately as well as combined company totals.

4.) Ability to generate one invoice for multiple station buys.

5.) Separate income statements by station and combined income statement for the company.

Neither traffic nor accounting system can meet the new criteria of your duopoly operation. The solution: Look at what is on the market and find a system that meets your new needs.

Independent But Consolidated

Scenario II. You are a large company and acquire additional stations in several markets, pairing them with existing properties in those same markets. Your goal is to leave each station independent and compete against each other, yet generate consolidated financial information.

Since each station within the market operates from different locations with heavy inventory demand, a single computerized traffic operation is inappropriate. You need to run two separate traffic operations and consolidate the balance sheet and income statement data at month-end. The solution: Put the traffic system you use in the newly acquired stations and set up modem communication to the corporate office.

Out With The Old ...

Scenario III. A large company, you acquire an additional AM/FM operation within the same market. While the goal is to eventually consolidate, the stations run separately for the first several months of operation.

The new acquisition has a different traffic and accounting system. While your current traffic system can handle some of your duopoly requirements, you aren't satisfied with the system's operation overall. In operating the stations separately, you discover that the new station's system can handle the duopoly operation and give you some of the features you are looking for. The solution: Keep the traffic system of the new acquisition because it meets more of your needs.

Start From Scratch

Remember that while your current system may be great for your operation now, it may not be able to handle the increased load of another station(s).

First, define the specific needs of the duopoly operation. Second, contact the different software vendors, even systems that you are not currently using. Be careful, keep an open mind and don't fall victim to the sales pitch.

Finally, find out how long the software vendor has been providing duopoly software. Many of the big names in the software field carry big price tags for the ability to handle additional stations.

Chapter 55

Setting Standards

Parenting Tips For Managers

By Chris Lytle

Good parents set standards for their children: No dessert until you finish your peas, one hour of television after your homework is finished, in bed with the lights out at nine o'clock sharp on school nights. Standards let children know what's expected and how well they are doing. The same is true of management's standards for salespeople. Setting new standards is the key to surpassing old limits.

- **Setting quantity standards isn't enough. They should be augmented with quality standards, timeliness standards and cost standards.**
- **An objective is what you expect to have accomplished in a set period of time; a standard is how that objective will be accomplished.**
- **Setting standards is as important to good management as it is to good parenting.**

Here are two important definitions:

1.) An objective is what you expect to have accomplished in a set period of time. Example: Increase billing by 20 percent per list over the next quarter.

2.) A standard is how that objective will be accomplished.

A New Set Of Standards

How do you achieve that 20 percent increase per list over the next quarter? You could require a quantity standard: X number of sales calls per day. However, it's possible for a salesperson to make the calls and still not meet the objective. Consider setting better quantity standards and then augmenting those with quality, timeliness and cost standards, too. Here are some examples:

Quantity Standards: Important Numbers

- Invest 15 minutes daily in planning and prioritizing your daily action list. Prepare a top 10 "hit list" or "most-wanted list" and keep it current. Plan calls on the top 10 every week. Complete a minimum of two database or consultant calls each week.

- Join at least one service club or professional organization to build your network.
- Send out five articles per week to clients and prospects. Send a minimum of three prospecting letters each week to people on your 10-most-wanted list.
- Schedule three breakfast meetings per week with clients.
- Get into a position each month to ask clients to invest four times more money than you need them to invest to make your quota.
- Expect to put in 50-55 hours per week.
- Have X percent or X dollars in local direct billing.

Quality Standards: No Typos

- Use the spell-checker function on your computer so you don't send out letters with typographical errors.
- Get your car washed once a week. Shine your shoes twice a week. Upgrade your business wardrobe.
- Read over the Instant Background of a business before you make a call, and prepare three questions based on your reading.
- Practice major presentations with the manager so you will be more relaxed during the actual sales call.

Timeliness Standards: Fast Follow-Up

- Make it a practice to arrive five minutes early for appointments.
- Follow up within three days of the schedule starting.
- Return every call within X minutes of receiving it.
- Convert database calls into written proposals within three to five business days.

Cost Standards: Conservation Of Resources

- Write orders on the rate card.
- Offer promotions and value-added only with orders of a certain amount and above.
- Recycle cassettes and conserve station supplies.
- Keep business meals to $X or pay the difference.
- Make multiple calls in a zone to maximize limited face-to-face selling time.

This is certainly not an exhaustive list — nor is every standard appropriate for every station or salesperson.

Chapter 56

De-Stressing Situations

Adapt, Alter And Avoid

By Mimi Donaldson

- **When you resist an event, you feel worry, anger and resentment.**
- **When you accept an event, you can stop, look at what you want and listen to your inner voice.**
- **Adapt yourself, alter the circumstance or avoid the stress.**

There you are — stuck in traffic — again. All the lanes are jammed, and you can't see anything! "I hate being behind a truck," your thought begins. You start to worry about being late. Your face feels hot; your right temple starts to throb. Just then, you hear a knocking sound coming from the engine. Is it the same knock that cost you $346 two weeks ago? On top of it all, it starts to drizzle — and traffic stops completely. "These people don't know how to drive in the rain!" you think, glaring at strangers in the next car. A scene of you arriving late starts playing in your head. You feel your neck and shoulders tighten; the throb in your right temple intensifies and spreads across your forehead. "My day is ruined," your internal voice declares.

And it may be. Stress is an internal response to an external event. The traffic jam is your external event, and all your responses are the ones you label "stress." Since the externals seldom change, how do we change our internal response? Pretend to love traffic jams? Not likely.

At WAR With Yourself

Stress is caused by resisting what's going on. When we resist a traffic jam or a rude person or an uncomfortable situation, we respond with three emotions: worry, anger and resentment.

Notice the first three letters of those words describe the stress response perfectly: WAR, the war within you. If you look at your stress event, you will find that the worry, anger and resentment are not caused by a traffic jam. The traffic jam is merely the trigger that sets off those three emotions inside you. Let's look at what they may be:

1.) You worry about being late — where are you going? To a beloved, joy-filled place? Or to a place you'd rather not go, where you feel anxiety and pressure to perform? What's this worry really about? Fear of reprisal, punishment? Perceived lack of choice on your part?

2.) You feel anger at the mechanic who fixed your car, suspecting he didn't really fix it. Is this suspicion familiar? Do you often mistrust people — and yourself? Or is your anger related to the notion that someone else should have chosen the mechanic or at least helped? Do you feel the duties you have in life are fairly distributed, or do you feel you do more than your share? This feeling can cause anger to many external stress "triggers."

3.) You feel resentment at "these people" who don't know how to drive as well as you do. Are you often impatient with people who don't do things exactly as you do? Do you resent the people in the supermarket who are standing in a faster-moving line?

The Pause That De-Stresses

How can we learn to stop fuming and seething in line, and become the person pleasantly chatting with another person?

Your first reaction is resistance. There is another reaction: the opposite of resist. Accept. I don't mean: "Oh, goody, a traffic jam, oh boy!" I mean: "Ah, a traffic jam. That's one of the things that drives me crazy, and here it is. " Use humor to accept. Only when you accept a situation can you act upon it. If you're busy resisting it, you're paralyzed.

When you accept, you can stop, look and listen. Stop means "push the pause button." You can use it to gain control over an automatic stress response. Look means recognize this is one of your stress triggers, and you have a choice about whether or not to get upset. Look also means look at what you really want and ask: "Is being stressed going to help me get it?" Listen means listen to your inner self, which tells you what to do.

There are three alternatives of action: adapt, alter and avoid. Using my "traffic jam" example, you can eliminate the third one right away — avoid.

Adapt means adapting yourself to the situation. Listen to entertaining audiotapes in traffic. The most useful adaptation is the car phone — albeit the most expensive.

Alter means changing the situation. Finding alternative routes to main roads, starting your journey sooner. Your inner voice will tell you to adapt, alter or avoid. And you will no longer be stressed.

Chapter 57

Computers And Lasers And Beepers
Oh My!

By Roy Pressman

- The latest technology should enhance your staff, not replace it.
- Voice mail can handle many more calls than a single operator, and messages are never missed.
- Word processing systems can increase staff efficiency.
- Dedicate one fax to outgoing and one to incoming faxes to smooth out any kinks in your faxing process.
- Digital beepers can notify staff of messages in their voice mail.

Society as a whole may not have reached George Orwell's prophesies, but the American office environment has come a long way in the last 10 years. Instead of typewriters, we now have word processors. Where there once was a receptionist, there is now an auto-attendant. Instead of memos, we get E-mail. And the message pad has been replaced by voice mail.

Computers have changed every aspect of the Radio station and have brought about a new breed of office equipment that can streamline your station. The latest technology will make your station's office staff more efficient, and it might even allow you to reduce staff members. But you should use this new technology to enhance your staff, not to replace it.

Also, don't exhaust your capital budget before you try your bartering skills. There are plenty of companies willing to trade for vmail, phone and computer systems.

What exactly does the new breed of office equipment do, and is it right for your station? The following may serve as a brief primer on the subject.

Press 1 For Sales ...

We've all heard of voice mail (vmail); in fact, you can't escape it. Vmail has become a part of our daily lives for two reasons: It can handle many more calls than a single operator, and messages are never missed. Vmail systems are usually made up of two separate parts: the auto-attendant and the voice mailbox system.

The auto-attendant answers the phone and routes the call to a particular extension, just as an operator does. If the extension is busy or the person doesn't answer, the call is transferred to the individual's voice mailbox. The caller hears a message from the person he or she is trying to reach and then leaves a detailed message. It's just like having an electronic answering machine at every employee's desk.

Voice mail systems work in conjunction with your phone system. Check with your phone company to see what type of phone system you have, because not all phone systems are compatible with a vmail system. "PBX" phone systems are usually compatible with vmail systems. (How can you tell if your phone system is a "PBX" type? If you have to dial 9 to get an outside extension, you probably have a PBX system.) This might be a great time to update your phone system!

Not all vmail systems are created equal. Look for a system that is efficient. You don't want your callers to press 20 numbers just to reach a person or a particular department. Make sure there is sufficient storage time to hold vmail messages. The number of calls that your vmail system can handle simultaneously is determined by the number of "ports" on your system. Purchase a system with enough ports to handle your phone traffic.

You don't have to use the auto-attendant feature all the time. Most stations still need to have a receptionist/operator at the front door, so have your receptionist answer all incoming calls. Use the vmail to take all messages. The auto-attendant can route calls after hours or, when too many calls come into the station at once, they can be routed to the auto-attendant.

Fax & Figures

The majority of fax machines utilize a thermal type of paper. Thermal printing leaves a lot to be desired, because the paper deteriorates after a period of time, so important faxes must be copied to plain paper.

Plain-paper faxes solve the thermal dilemma. Although they've been around for about four years, prices have been high until recently. Now, not only have prices of the fax machines dropped, the cost of receiving each fax (paper, toner, ink cartridge) has dropped.

How do you know if you're using a thermal fax? Look for a roll of paper in the fax machine. Thermal fax machines use a heat process — there's no ink or printing cartridge. Plain-paper fax machines use either a toner cartridge, an ink cartridge or a film cartridge. Some machines can hold 500 sheets of paper.

Set up at least two fax machines in your facility. Dedicate one fax to outgoing and one to incoming faxes. This can greatly smooth out any kinks in your faxing process.

Hello Word Processor ... Goodbye Typewriter

If your staff composes letters or writes copy on a typewriter, you're in the Stone Age! Typewriters are great for typing cart labels or a quick envelope, but if you really want to be efficient, replace your typewriters with a word processing system. Install a computer network that will allow your staff to share resources and printers. To speed up the printing process, use laser printers with at least eight-pages-per-minute speed. If your office is large, install several laser printers so that work doesn't get bogged down.

Give all your salespeople digital beepers, which display the number to call back. When used in conjunction with a vmail system, the beepers can notify salespeople of their messages. You might want to look into the new type of alpha-numeric beeper system, which sends actual text messages to sales/engineering people in the field.

Sort, Staple & Feed

How many copies do you make in one month? How critical is the speed of the machine (copies per minute)? Do you need an automatic sorter/stapler? These are questions that your equipment supplier will ask you. There are usually two charges involved: the price of the machine and the price of the maintenance contract. Maintenance contract prices are usually tied to the monthly number of copies. Machine prices vary with copy speed, duty cycle (the recommended per-month limit of copies) and special features. If you do a lot of copying, make sure the machine can handle the load. If speed is a factor, select a machine that can do at least 60 copies per minute.

Chapter 58

RoboStation:
The Next Evolution Of Traffic And Billing Software?

By Katy Bachman

Perhaps the biggest attraction of LMAs or duopolies is the prospect of increasing cash flow by eliminating or combining redundant departments. The potential cost efficiencies have led broadcasters to re-examine every function at their Radio stations. Such evaluation has typically grouped the back office into one of three categories: crucial, unnecessary or — as many operators are finding — capable of being automated.

- **Before you automate your operations, define your problem. Remember that every station has different needs and applications.**
- **Make sure the system is easy to learn — and easy to train new people how to use.**
- **Don't fall for a system just because it has all the bells and whistles; they might be bells and whistles you'll never need.**
- **Be sure you understand the fee schedule completely — and whether upgrades carry an additional cost.**
- **Check out the company. Is this its main business or just a sideline? Seek a list of satisfied customers.**
- **Make sure the system meets your needs before you buy it.**

Depending on the structure of the LMA or duopoly, however, recombining administrative functions — particularly traffic and billing — can be challenging. Virtually all software and hardware suppliers have encountered significant hurdles in developing product that adequately serves the traffic and billing needs of broadcasters, largely because of the specific configuration of each duopoly or LMA situation.

"The variety of combinations seems endless, which initially posed a problem for traffic and billing software companies," says Debbie Hamby, sales manager for Datacount of Opelika, Alabama. "Broadcasters had a need to group stations together, sell all inventory together, schedule under a common order, bill for all stations under a common invoice and run reports combined."

While upper-level management might not always keep it top-of-mind, the traffic department is vital to running a Radio station. The traffic manager ensures that advertisers get what they paid for, and ultimately makes sure that advertisers pay for what they get. "Traffic is the most important function in the smooth running of a Radio station," says Adrian Charlton, general manager of software provider The Management.

Thom Mead, support manager for Register Data Systems (RDS), agrees. "Traffic is the most stepped-on, and the most powerful, position at a Radio station," he says. "The traffic manager often can tick off every advertiser a station has."

Since its introduction in the early 1980s, traffic and billing software has helped stations more efficiently deal with one half of the Radio business: tracking sales, scheduling commercials and billing advertisers. But until recently, the only way to reconcile what was planned with what actually aired still required generating another log through the programming department. Any amount of automated information churned out by the traffic and billing department was useless if the programming log had to be keyed into the traffic and billing system.

Closing "The Loop"

Enter digital audio automation, which allows computers to communicate with each other. Today, few broadcasters will even look at a traffic and billing system if it doesn't share information with the audio (music and programming) system, a fact that has led many software companies to develop their own digital audio systems. Among these are RDS' Phantom, Radio Computing Systems' Linker and The Management's Digital DJ. Other firms such as Datacount, Columbine, Computer Concepts and Custom Business Systems Inc. have developed software that "talks" to the major (if not all) audio systems available today. For example, Datacount's DARTS system uses an "Automatic Log Reconciliation" feature that allows the station to download its traffic and billing log to Arrakis' DigiLink or more than a dozen other audio systems, and then upload it for complete reconciliation of both logs.

"The trend is to computerize the entire station with traffic at the center," says The Management's Charlton.

To this end, Columbine has recently introduced two new modules to its automation system: Sales Analysis and Credit Management Plus.

"The emphasis in the future will be on decision support information, not just logging and billing," says Mike Oldham, director of sales and marketing for Columbine. "The systems will need to help stations do more than just perform functions; they'll need to help stations make better management decisions."

Radio Computing Services Inc. claims to be the only firm seriously marketing a total system that could truly turn your station into RoboStation. When RCS purchased Decision Inc., a traffic and billing software firm, and added its "Master Control" product, it had gathered all the pieces to build "RCS Works." The system combines all production, programming, traffic, research, billing and sales functions.

"We've tried to eliminate all paperwork at the Radio station by making all reports available instantly on screen," says RCS President Andrew Economos. "RCS Works" is a complete workstation, but it also is modular, according to Economos. Buyers can purchase individual elements or the whole works, but no one yet is using the entire workstation.

Still, many industry observers believe it won't be long before RoboStations become the norm.

"Advancements have lowered the cost of computers and made them more powerful, so that it's easier to move huge files like music, making the unified system more a reality," says Economos. "Today, we can store a song for $10.50 compared to a cart, which can store a song for $8.50. It's getting closer."

Selecting a traffic and billing system for Radio isn't much different from selecting software for your home or business computer. Individual work habits or needs are a highly personal consideration, even in the workplace. Fortunately, some 47 companies are marketing a wide variety of software that can be applied to specific station requirements. Therefore, it is important to look before you leap to integrate and automate all the functions at your station. "RoboStation" can be designed to handle virtually all business operations, but a little human brainpower up front can set everything right before the switch is ever flipped.

All Things Considered

• Before you do anything, define your problem. Decide what you want to accomplish. If you seek advice from other stations, remember that they may have different needs and applications. If you want software only for certain station functions, concentrate on your needs. Every operation does not have to be "RoboStation" and, in some cases, it might be cheaper not to automate everything.

• The person(s) who will be using the system should be a big part of the decision. Usually, that's the traffic person. The reality with the traffic department, however, is that it often has the highest turnover at the station. Whatever system you decide to purchase, make sure it will be easy for the next person to learn. Also remember that what seems easy for one person might not be easy for the next.

"We've found that putting our software into Windows makes it easier to train those who will be using it — and makes the information more accessible to more people at the station," says Columbine's Oldham. Though the company has yet to convert its entire system to Windows, its latest modules have been. Windows, of course, also is offered by other software vendors.

Training is important and, in many cases, it could be the most important feature of any software system. Find out if the software company provides it, and what it charges. Some companies charge anywhere from $250 to $500 a day plus expenses, and many training programs can take weeks. Find out what arrangements can be made for additional training services if you get a new traffic person later on.

• Don't be wowed by technology alone; in other words, don't fall for a system just because it has all the bells and whistles. They could be bells and whistles you'll never need.

• Determine your budget in advance. Fortunately, fierce competition and finite demand have kept prices reasonable. Virtually every software company wants to do business with you, so you have some room for negotiation. Prices are set according to a number of variables, including the number of stations you intend to run off the system. Be sure you understand the fee schedule completely.

System upgrades or additional features may also add to the cost of a system. Some companies charge for the upgrade, while others may have a quarterly charge for any improvements or upgrades. Again, be sure to ask.

• If you upgrade your hardware, make sure it remains compatible with your traffic and billing software. Digital audio companies are breeding fast. Some traffic and billing companies provide their own digital audio hardware systems. Others don't, but will talk to a variety of systems.

• Consider time and growth. Where do you intend to be a few years down the line? Many managers believe that LMAs and duopolies are such a powerful force in the future of Radio that if you are not involved in one today, you could be in one tomorrow. Therefore, whatever system you buy today should be able to handle the total number of stations you plan to operate. Also, if you plan to automate other functions of your stations, it will be crucial that the systems can communicate.

If you're leaning toward the "RoboStation" route, or expect to in the future, try to anticipate all your needs in advance. Nothing is more frustrating than buying a new system, only to find that you still have to stop everything and complete some tasks manually.

• Check out the company. Does it have experience running, managing and working in Radio? Is it a stable company with a strong list of customers? Consider whether or not traffic and billing software is its main business or just a sideline. Like it or not, the company you choose will be a partner in your future. Always ask for a list of satisfied customers — and call them for input. Be sure to ask about customer support and service.

• Finally, see for yourself. Go to demonstrations at conventions. Play with the equipment before you buy it. Try several different systems. Don't wait for the hardware to be installed before you discover it doesn't meet your needs.

Chapter 59

Let Your Stars Shine

The Challenge Of Managing Big Talent

By Walter Sabo

Many stations are winning their competitive battles with high-priced, high-profile air talent. For general managers, personality programming presents a challenge. Since most GMs come from sales rather than programming, they likely have had little daily contact with the medium's stars. Yet, effective management of big-ego, big-ticket talent is essential to reap the ratings benefits. It's a fact of the business: The bigger your stars, the bigger your profits.

- **Air talent works for recognition. You must provide constant, positive feedback.**
- **Comments must be consistent. Limit criticisms to one per day.**
- **When listeners or clients complain, it means they're listening, but they are not representative of your audience. Do not pass these complaints along to talent.**
- **Never deny stars their stardom.**

I have worked with or managed personalities such as Casey Kasem, Dr. Ruth Westheimer, Sally Jessy Raphael, John Gambling, Dr. Don Rose, Dan Daniel, Rick Shaw and dozens of other legends. Plus, I've had the privilege of helping to develop tomorrow's legends such as John Kobylt and Ken Chiampou of KFI and formerly of "New Jersey 101.5." Now that I've dropped some names, let me pass along some advice:

• *Understand vulnerability.* Imagine you're sitting at your desk, writing a memo. You make a mistake, throw it away and start again. However, instead of making the mistake privately, you are recorded by a TV camera. A tape recorder is recording every call. Your boss and your boss' spouse are monitoring your every move via a direct line to their office and home. Just as you start to throw away the errant memo, your phone rings. It's your boss … wanting to talk about the mistake you just made.

Now you are beginning to understand what it's like to be on the air.

Air talents' exposure puts them in a constant state of vulnerability. To keep them performing at their best, it is necessary to make them feel secure. Here's how to achieve that goal:

Filling The Feedback Void

• *More than for money, air talent works for recognition.* Since there is no studio audience, they are performing in a void — a void that management must fill. A salesman might work harder if he doesn't get an immediate compliment from you. An air talent will think he is about to be fired.

An air personality who does not receive constant, positive feedback from the boss will do anything to get attention. Bad things. Anything for feedback. Then, at contract time, they will make considerable monetary demands to compensate for the lack of applause. One simple thank-you note can save hundreds of thousands of dollars in compensation. (If you don't believe that, then you don't have a clue about talent ego.)

• *Be consistent.* Lacking a live audience, your air personalities place enormous weight on your comments. Your expressed likes and dislikes must be consistent day after day. Good rule: Only one criticism a day. A long list of concerns will crush the talent's ego, and they will not be able to do anything right.

• *When listeners call and complain, it's working!* There are 30 to 40 stations in your market. For listeners to recall anything is a miracle. Who would write or call a Radio station regarding matters of individual taste? Certainly not an active young adult with a full life, children and a job. Those letters come from non-representative people.

For every strong complaint you receive, there is at least one listener with a strong positive reaction. Do not — I repeat — do not tell the talent about complaint calls. Ever. When you relate listener complaints, talent assumes you agree with the complaint. And they think they are about to be fired.

Talent Is The Star

• *Never deny stars their stardom.* To 99 percent of the population, all they know about your station is what they hear on the air. Not your memos, not your lobby decor. Talent is the Radio station.

Misguided managers have been known to say to talent: "The Radio station is the star." That's like saying to a salesperson: "You should work for free." To inspire talent to kill for you, give them their stardom. Unlike some other employees, air talent will not take advantage of that knowledge; they will appreciate it.

• *Involve talent in the programming process.* Air talent has valuable knowledge. They know what makes the phones ring. They know what listeners remember about the station. Before making a major programming change, talk it over with the talent. It will help them buy into the change and could prevent a costly mistake.

• *Do not expect talent to work eight hours a day inside the station.* Great talent has the ability to talk one-on-one to listeners about their immediate interests and needs. That skill comes from constant, personal contact with listeners. A talent who spends most of the day inside the station with Radio people cannot possibly talk to listeners effectively.

Understand how much time and emotional energy a good talent puts into a show. They read all the papers, watch all the mass-appeal TV shows and attend community events. When talent does those things, they are doing their job.

Some managers who have never been on the air have the notion that during records, the talent isn't doing much work. Do one air shift yourself and you will extinguish that misconception immediately.

Who's Listening?

• *Your friends and family are not normal.* The moment a friend knows you're in Radio, they listen harder. They remember more. They want to be able to talk to you about your work when they see you. You'll lose the respect of the air staff if you quote your spouse or friend's feelings about the programming. The air staff won't know whom to please — you or your friends.

• *Your sales personnel and their clients are not normal listeners.* Their job is to field complaints and defend the station. Any smart client trying to negotiate a better rate will have complaints about talent content. Complaints from clients mean they're listening to your station — and the AE should thank them!

• *Follow the chain of command.* The GM should never use the hotline unless the talent is breaking the law or drunk. And then only if he or she cannot reach the PD.

• *Smile when you walk by the studio.* The person on the air is performing, but there's no audience. If you're not smiling when you walk by, the air talent assumes you are listening to the show and frowning about something you've heard. In a fever, they ask other staffers: "Is he mad at me?"

• *Publicly celebrate all victories.* When an air talent is quoted in the paper, makes a good personal appearance or has a strong book, make a big deal out of it. Give out plaques. Let the entire staff know who the star is. This type of recognition makes air talent more, not less, manageable.

Chapter 60

Passion Plays
. . . And Pays

By Richard Chapin

- **Radio stations can capture listener loyalty and passion by offering something different from the rest.**
- **Great managers know that just going along does not appeal to the souls and hearts of their listeners.**
- **The passion philosophy applies to sales, too. Great salespeople have a passion for finding out what their clients like and dislike.**

Ted Bolton made some important observations regarding passion in Radio programming (*Radio Ink*, Aug. 9, 1993) in a Marketing column. I agree, and I feel strongly that passion should be present in sales as well.

The "herding instincts" in Radio management are indeed making this an "industry of sheep." If you get in your car and head out on the interstate from somewhere in the east and just drive west, you'll hear a sameness that is sickening. What's the answer?

In my early days, there weren't that many stations. People could get large shares of listening. Not so today. As observers keep telling us, there isn't very much ratings difference between first place and the sixth or seventh station in the top 150 markets. Competition has led to compression. So what should we be doing?

The good Radio manager today will work hard trying to find out what the audience really likes or dislikes. You have to work on people's emotions. If you do the right job, you'll be remembered when your audience is called on to say which station they like or dislike.

I've seen firsthand examples where Radio stations have captured the passion of their listeners. Hot new country KFRG in San Bernardino has captured its market. Why? Because it was different and created passion in its listeners. Look at "The Point" in St. Louis. They created a new sense of discovery and filled a void for their younger listeners. These stations, and many others, are going to exist on the passion and the loyalty of their listeners.

Great Radio stations are challenging their audiences every day by coming up with something new and blending it with what has been done in the past and what they think the future will be. Great managers know that just going along does not capture the souls and hearts of their audience.

Translate this philosophy to sales. The really great salespeople today have a passion for what they do. They are working hard at trying to find out what their advertising clients really want. They have a passion to be inquisitive. And they have a passion for Radio. If we don't have a passion for our work, if we don't have a passion for our station, then how are we going to lead?

I think today that the passionate salespeople need to work with passionate programmers to create something different, something on the cutting edge, something that will be remembered most when a listener or a client thinks about a Radio station.

Chapter 61

The Single Most Important Management Technique

Appreciation Breeds Success

By Rick Ott

Recently, a general manager asked me if I thought there existed one single most important management technique that, when implemented correctly, would make him and his station highly successful. There is, and it's as simple and easy to use as it is powerful: Make people feel good about themselves.

- **When you make people feel good about themselves, you awaken their zest for life and work, which makes them more productive and loyal.**
- **Express appreciation. Employees value this above money and all else.**
- **Strengthen camaraderie with careful wording. Use "you" with praise but "we" and "let's" in reviewing mistakes.**
- **Praise employees' decision-making abilities and they will start making better decisions.**

When you make people feel good about themselves on a regular basis, a wealth of magical things happen, such as:

• Morale heightens. When people feel good about themselves, they're happier, more cooperative and less problematic.

• Productivity rises. People work harder, with genuine interest and concern.

• Loyalty abounds. When you make people feel good about themselves, they'll do almost anything for you.

• Turnover declines. People hesitate to leave when they're into a good thing.

• You attract the best job candidates. Word gets out that your station is a great place to work, and great workers are lined up to get in.

• Your bottom line just keeps getting better. With the preceding five advantages kicking in, how can you help but outperform the competition and profit immensely?

Why It Works

Making people feel good about themselves is powerful, motivating stuff. We are all born with an instinctively high belief in ourselves. Only by living and learning (oftentimes incorrectly), do we begin to doubt ourselves. When we find someone who recognizes our abilities, believes in us and encourages us, we suddenly feel in harmony with our innermost instincts. That person awakens our zest for life and work.

How To Do It

You're familiar with the notion of "catching people doing something right" and administering praise. Good start. But there's more to it than that. Here are three specific techniques for making people feel good about themselves that you should use regularly:

• *Express appreciation.* Use that exact word — appreciation — in some form. "I really appreciate your taking responsibility and seeing this matter through," "I appreciate your help with this," "I have a strong appreciation for your talent," are a few examples. Remember, the thing employees cherish most from an employer, above money and all else, is appreciation for their work.

You can take it one step further on occasion and express appreciation for the fact that they're here in the first place. "We're very fortunate to have you on the staff" is an empowering statement.

• *Use wording that strengthens camaraderie.* People want to be an important part of the station; they want a strong sense of contribution and belonging. Let people know they are an integral part of the whole. Do this by selecting your words carefully in regular conversation. For example, use the word "you" when soliciting their opinion ("What do you think of … ") and praising ("You did a great job with … "). But use the words "we," "us" and "let's" when talking about taking action ("Perhaps we should go about it this way … ") or when reviewing a mistake ("Here's where we may have gone wrong. Let's try this instead … "). The idea is to strengthen the bond between employees and the station as a whole, rather than hanging them out alone to fend for themselves in a hostile environment.

• *Praise their decision-making ability.* We live each day making numerous decisions. Some small, some big. Some prove profitable, others mistakes. Regardless of how things turn out later, we want to believe we're making good decisions at the time we make them. Most of the time, people really do make good decisions. It's just that the bad ones get most of the attention. Here's where you come in. Tell people they make good decisions. Tell them you admire their reasoning and decision-making ability. When you tell people they make good decisions, they will, in fact, start making better decisions. They want to live up to your belief, and they're going to give it extra effort to make sure they don't destroy that belief.

Chapter 62

Promoting From Within
The 36 Most Important Questions To Ask
By Dave Gifford

> **• If you don't ask the right questions, the blame for hiring errors is yours.**

You have decided to hire a new sales manager and to promote from within, but you are undecided as to which of two candidates to appoint. Of the 95 questions I used to ask, below are the 36 most important questions:

1.) What are your career goals?

2.) Describe, in detail, your plan for achieving those goals.

3.) Are you willing to make less money to get into management? Why?

4.) What does it take to be a world-class sales manager?

5.) What particular strengths do you have that transfer?

6.) What do you think you would like most about being a sales manager?

7.) What do you think you would like least about being a sales manager?

8.) Which of your colleagues could you work for if I chose them over you?

9.) Who wouldn't you work for?

What If?

10.) Would you be willing to take this position knowing that you would be fired if you fail to achieve the station's sales targets?

11.) If you failed as sales manager, would you be willing to take over a list and go back on the street?

12.) Here are my three major problems with you as a salesperson: a. b. c. How would you manage a salesperson with the very same problems?

13.) What can't you manage from Giff's job description for a sales manager? (Chapter Two)

14.) Do you have any requirements of me as "minimum requirements" for taking this position?

15.) What is your philosophy of how to make money in this business?

16.) What are your ideas for outselling the competition?

17.) What would you change if I did give you the job?

18.) What do the salespeople complain about the most, and how would you address those complaints?

19.) How would you handle the _____ situation? (Note: In asking how they would handle given situations, it is critical that you prepare several real-world examples you're both familiar with. It is your single strongest line of questioning.)

Managing Colleagues

20.) What is your philosophy of managing people?

21.) If I choose you, how will you win the respect of your colleagues?

22.) What if they reject you?

23.) Which of your fellow salespeople match the following profiles: Superstar? Star? Future star? Fading star? Uncommitted star? High producer? Mid producer? Low producer? Failing salesperson?

24.) What would be your criteria for firing a salesperson?

25.) Whom would you let go? Why?

26.) How would you manage ____? (Note: Ask of each fellow salesperson.)

27.) If you get this job, you're likely to end up either "too nice" or "too tough" as a manager; which side are you likely to fall on? Why?

28.) How would you get the salespeople to make more presentations and more first-time-ever opportunity calls?

29.) How would you get the salespeople to go after more new business?

Motivation & Persuasion

30.) How would you get the salespeople to sell further in advance and go after more long-term business?

31.) How would you go about increasing our average unit rate?

32.) Sometime in the next 24 hours, I want you to interview me two times ... once as a candidate with Radio sales experience and once as a candidate with no experience whatsoever.

33.) Describe the kind of indoctrination training program that you would institute for new salespeople.

34.) How much time, in order to "manage by example," do you

think a sales manager should commit weekly to personal sales?

35. How much time would you commit weekly to helping the salespeople open as well as close sales?

36. Here are my three biggest concerns in giving you this position: a., b., c.

Persuade me not with promises, but with facts and examples of your abilities as they translate to the job requirements of a sales manager.

Chapter 63

Pea-Eyes: A Revenue Source By Any Other Name ...

Would Still Make Money

By Mike McDaniel

- **Per-inquiry or direct response has gotten a bad rap as a revenue source over the years. Actually, it's a moneymaker.**
- **By using per-inquiry advertising on unsold air, the station has no investment to lose.**
- **Some PI firms pay even if your listeners call only for information on a product.**

This space is dedicated to making money for broadcasters. Radio broadcasters in particular, but many of the promotions featured will work for TV and cable, too. Radio stations throughout the country have different ways of generating revenue. One threw out the rate card and sells only packages; another does all promotions. Yet another just keeps hiring salespeople until the numbers fit.

There is another form of revenue that has been around for a long time, an income source that is perhaps the most misunderstood concept of all time. PIs. Pea-Eyes, short for per-inquiry. Because PIs have gotten such a bad rap over the years, industry moguls have tried to soften the hurt with a new moniker: direct response. Call them what you will, they are moneymakers.

Nothing To Lose

Every Radio station has unsold airtime. And when that time passes, it has no value. The inventory has to be sold at rate before use, or marked down and packaged before the time comes or it is lost. That's where PIs come into play. With per-inquiry advertising, the Radio station broadcasts commercials requiring a direct response from the listener. Often an 800 number; sometimes mail. When the listener buys, the station is paid a commission on the sale, not a per-spot rate.

Mr. Negative will surely say: "Yeah, but you end up running 264 spots for some sport magazine and sell one subscription for $6.25." If you had commission-only salespeople working for you and they did not deliver, you would get others, right? Same with PIs. There is no way to know which ones will produce until you try them. But since you are using unsold air, you have no investment. Nothing to lose, everything to gain.

At a recent meeting of broadcasters, the question was asked: "Who runs PIs?" The results were not unexpected. One said they made his station sound trashy; another said his accountant didn't like them because he preferred to assign a dollar amount to every spot run. The excuses went on and on until one admitted he made more than $2,000 last month with PIs. Trashy? Probably not.

Major PI Players

There are several major players in the market, all with stables of product; some even pay if your listeners just call for more information. One pays $64 for every information request call. Most average about 25 percent to 35 percent of the retail price paid to the station.

"So you don't forget, order before midnight tonight, here's how to order ..." PIs have been around on TV forever. (Ted Turner built his empire on PIs.) Here is a partial list of PI vendors. Call and ask for a list of products and payouts, and get on your way to big bucks from unsold airtime.

- Lawrence Butner Advertising 212-682-3200
- Phase IV Productions 414-921-0351
- Springside Marketing 717-898-9191
- Direct Response Broadcast Network 215-925-8585
- Target & Response 312-573-0500
- Media Advantage 201-325-0050
- Marina Advertising 310-578-1660
- Encore Inc. 502-499-1556
- The Radio Store 812-847-9830
- Dave Burns (Bose) 317-935-7087

My experience shows that the dishonorable PI companies of the past have faded, and new, reputable companies have taken their place. These new companies provide computerized lists of responses and are anxious to see stations succeed, because it means future business. If you're operating on assumptions about past PI advertising, it's worth exploring again. Today, it can be an excellent and reliable revenue source.

(If you are using PI companies not listed here, or if you're in the PI business, we want to hear from you. We want to hear about your successes and failures and share your reactions to those first big checks.)

Chapter 64

Taming The Maintenance Monster

Budgeting For The Unknown Expense

By Roy Pressman

It's impossible to know exactly how much money you will spend in one year for engineering expenses. Certain expenses are unavoidable, but how do we plan and budget properly? If a transmitter failure makes you spend more money than your budget allows, would you wait until Jan. 1 to go back on the air? With a little organization and planning, you can ensure that your engineering budget is sufficient to keep your facility going.

- **You can set up a budget with sufficient funds to properly maintain your facility.**
- **Review your equipment failure rates on a yearly basis and make budget adjustments accordingly.**
- **You can budget for energy costs based on the previous year's bill. To reduce electricity costs, consider an energy audit by the power company or an independent firm.**
- **Air conditioning, telephone, computer systems and generators all require regular servicing to maintain reliability.**

Prepare For Repairs

First of all, have your engineer compile a list of the station's equipment in a computer database such as DBASE III. The exact computer program is not important; just get the information entered into the computer. Make sure that every piece of equipment in your facility is included.

Now, enter the exact known cost of maintaining each piece of equipment. (For example: Pinch rollers for cart machines need to be replaced every six months to a year, etc.) Next, enter the cost of possible major repairs, based on major component failure, for each piece of equipment. Set up a separate parts budget to cover any minor equipment repairs.

When you've compiled your list, get a total amount — and don't faint. You won't need major repairs on each piece of equipment each year. Your facility will have a certain failure rate, and you need to guess what yours will be. A good place to start is 30 percent. Take the total from your database and multiply it by 30 percent. After one year, you might need to adjust this failure rate depending on your facility.

Power Bills

You can easily budget your energy consumption by reviewing the previous year's power bills. If the power company hasn't changed its rates, month-by-month power consumption should track closely year to year.

Electricity costs can be reduced. Consider an energy audit by your local power company or an independent consultant. Look at your power bills and then compare them to other Radio facilities' power usage. Most power bills show kilowatt usage and/or demand, which makes a comparison very easy. If your power meter incorporates a demand meter, you are charged a premium when you need more power. Ask your engineer to run only one transmitter at a time. Test the backup transmitter directly on the air (not into a dummy load) or, if your facility has an emergency generator, test the backup transmitter when the generator is on-line. If the generator is on-line, you are not using the power company's resources and the demand meter will show no change. The whole idea is to reduce the amount of energy you demand from the power company at one moment. You'd be surprised how much money this can save!

Power companies sometimes offer different rate structures to large power consumers, and this also can save you big $$$. Check with your power company to see if you qualify for one of these bulk rates.

Service Contracts — Friend Or Foe?

Service contracts are great because they tell you exactly what the costs will be to maintain several areas of your facility, but they're not cheap. Some contracts include labor only, so make sure to budget extra money for parts. Your vendor should be able to supply you with a guesstimate of the yearly parts costs. Service contracts usually cover the following areas: air conditioning, telephone systems, computer systems, generators and office equipment.

Air Conditioning

To have a reliable air conditioning system, the AC units must be checked monthly and the air filters must be changed. This is best done by a qualified air conditioning company, and an AC service contract usually includes these services. Be careful: Most AC service contracts are labor only. Make sure your contract includes 24-hour service in case of emergencies. Depending on your transmitter site, lack of AC can put you off the air and damage your equipment. Your on-air personalities aren't going to be performing at their best in a studio that's 95 degrees. Prevent catastrophes by installing redundant AC units at the studio and transmitter site.

You can significantly reduce your power bill by installing energy-efficient AC units at the studio and transmitter site.

Telephone Systems

Don't bog down your engineering department with telephone repairs; invest in service contracts for your telephone system. A service agreement will get you back up and running quickly and will shield you from unexpected maintenance costs. Larger phone systems should have a parts and labor contract.

Computer Systems

Computer system service contracts are usually expensive and sometimes unnecessary. If your facility uses IBM-compatible computers, your engineer can stock a total complement of replacement parts at a fraction of the cost of a service contract. If a particular computer is critical to your station, then you might consider keeping a complete backup unit or a service contract on the particular unit.

Generators

If you have a generator at your transmitter site, you most likely have one at your studio location plant. These generators need weekly maintenance or they'll fail when most needed. Have your generators serviced on a parts-and-labor basis, and schedule one major service per year. Your generator company can give you an idea of the yearly costs for this type of schedule. Your engineering department would test all generators on a weekly basis and then log the results of the tests.

A Radio station is no different from a car: With proper preventive maintenance and a good mechanic, it can run for years. Give your engineering department the tools needed to keep the facility running smoothly. And use service companies in areas that are out of your engineering department's expertise.

Chapter 65

Ask Questions Now

Save Money Later

By George Whitaker

In dealing with engineering personnel, I have two suggestions: Don't be in too big a hurry, and ask lots of questions.

- **On engineering projects, two important points to remember are: Don't be in a hurry, and ask lots of questions.**
- **The planning stage is the important time to ask questions, so that the actual project runs smoothly and at the least cost.**
- **The manager does not need to get involved in technical details, but a basic understanding can help answer the question: Is this a good investment?**

The old adage "Haste makes waste" certainly applies to Radio station projects. The projects where I have seen the most waste of time and money have been the ones where they wanted it done yesterday.

Following are a couple of examples of both ways of doing things from my tenure with the Rodriguez stations.

The month after I arrived on the job, I was shown a building, a former insurance office, on Monday and was told to move the station into it by the next Saturday. By working almost every hour of the next five days, I did have them in by the weekend. However, in analyzing the event over a period of time, I estimated that we spent at least $10,000 needlessly.

At that time, I did not know the owner, Marcos, well enough to talk to him, and I simply did what the manager told me to do. In later years, I showed him my analysis of the project and he was astounded at how much money had been poured down a rathole. I have always been extremely conservative but, when you are pressed for time, you do what is expedient without considering cost.

Planning Pays

The really important time should be the planning stage. Once a project starts, it should move quickly, smoothly and at the least cost to accomplish your goals. This goes hand in hand with asking lots of questions. This is the kind of rapport Marcos and I developed later. We would go over a project with each of us asking questions of the other.

Let me cite an example of the way it should work:

We constructed a four-tower array in east Dallas in 1989. By this time, Marcos and I talked almost daily, and we hashed this project out thoroughly before beginning construction.

We proceeded to go over every item from land preparation to tying down the last wire and turning it on. I asked him questions about what he wanted in terms of investment. In other words: If we use solid rod towers instead of tubing, do you think it will make the station worth more? How showy do you think the transmitter building ought to be? Do you think we should fence the entire area or just the towers? How much security system do you think we need? We went through hundreds of questions like these, with him asking me to provide the alternatives for each item. We spent hours and hours doing this, but he got just what he wanted as an investment, and I got a transmitter site that has gotten a number of compliments from visiting engineers. Plus, when all was said and done, we spent about $75,000 less than the original estimate.

The All-Important Question

The manager does not need to get into really technical questions. However, if you have a basic understanding of the workings, you can help with the all-important question: Is it a good investment? Some things, of course, are mandatory and we have no choice. For instance, you can't decide not to put up fencing at all. However, at every turn there are questions that can lead to saving money. Solid vs. tubular towers is an example. Other things to consider are: Would we want to build our own tuning boxes? What other means can we use to accomplish the same thing?

On a number of occasions, I would think that I had considered all the ways to do something and would be prepared to implement my ideas. But then the question "Aren't there any other alternatives?" would start me thinking again, and I would find that there was indeed a better way.

A manager who learns to ask the right questions is not only going to save money but is much more enjoyable to work for. And, the manager's assistance in making the decisions removes a lot of the pressure from the engineer.

Chapter 66

Sorry, Wrong Future

Do Technology Suppliers Have The Wrong Vision Of Radio?

By Marty Gould

My first NAB Radio Show in several years was an interesting, educational experience. I went to Dallas for a specific purpose: to get enough answers to my questions regarding digital/computer automation to make a sensible purchase decision. After all, this will be the single largest capital investment we'll ever make. It's a decision that could not be made from a brochure. The NAB Radio Show was the perfect place to gather information, make comparisons, see the differences and make good deals.

- **Despite the futuristic displays, few suppliers are actually addressing the needs of a changing Radio industry.**
- **Although news/talk is among the fastest-growing formats in the industry, there were only about two suppliers at the NAB show capable of addressing the complex needs of the format.**
- **Only one supplier was found to handle the needs of three stations operating three formats out of one facility, an increasingly common combination.**

After three dizzying days of flashy computer screens, pseudo-futuristic furniture, bright lights and buzzwords, I compiled some observations, in the hopes of taking home from Dallas more than just my pile of complimentary magazines and bag full of premium items.

I was relieved and fortified to meet other owners and managers who came to NAB to discover the same things. Dozens of broadcasters, large market and small, all talking about their need to streamline operations, automate repetitive tasks, make their stations more simple to operate, save money.

Many had stations just like mine: a music-oriented FM, paired with a news/talk AM. Some were in the process of acquiring third and fourth stations in their markets. The rest were planning for it down the line. No one was standing still. Every broadcaster I talked to expressed the same purpose for being in Dallas: preparing for the future.

We also shared the same fears. Which one of us would make the mistake of buying a dinosaur? Could any of us really afford to make a $50,000 mistake?

Fascinating And Frustrating

My partners and I spent months preparing for this adventure, analyzing our own particular needs, learning how the technology worked, trying to sort out help from hype. We came armed with pages of specific questions about how any particular system could solve our problems.

How fascinating the exhibition floor was. Fascinating and frustrating. We spent hours moving from display to display, grilling salespeople, getting answers. To our delight, we think we found what we were looking for. To our dismay, we discovered many companies pretending to sell solutions to our problems, but incapable of actually solving them.

Despite all the futuristic displays, I was struck by the fact that many of these companies were still facing backward, trying to make 1990s technology fit into a 1970s definition of Radio: disc jockey as the center of the universe.

As a group of us wandered around the hall, we had a clear picture in our mind of the future, and it didn't include a 20-year-old disc jockey sitting in a studio segueing songs and firing off commercials from a computer. Our future doesn't even have disc jockeys. That doesn't mean we plan on turning our stations into automated "jukeboxes." It simply means there are new, different and better ways of "manufacturing" our product.

Many of the suppliers who are marketing digital equipment at the NAB Radio Show have only two visions of the future. One: a disc jockey doing a daily shift in a high-tech studio. The other: an automated station on a satellite music service. My stations don't fit either of those visions. Most stations don't. A casual walk around the convention center proved that.

A visitor couldn't go 10 feet without bumping into another "nationally syndicated talk show host."

Thousands of Radio stations are airing dozens of these programs. Many stations take feeds from different networks, juggling satellite channels all day long. Each station stitches together its own day of programming, based on what's best for its market and competitive situation.

From my understanding, news/talk is the third most programmed format in the United States. Now, guess how many digital computer systems we found on the exhibition floor that were able to accommodate the multiple switching and feed delays of a complex news/talk format?

By my count, just two. Some digital suppliers, when asked, couldn't even figure out how to record and play back long-form programming (an hour or longer).

The Search For Solutions

The promises of cost savings and improved operation evaporated when the realities of our current situations conflicted with a supplier's vision: a backward look at the way Radio was.

What if your station programs its own music? Most stations still do and will continue to do so. Reliable music playback, seamless interface with traffic and music software, and digital commercial storage are all key factors in deciding what system to buy.

How many suppliers did we find that were able to handle all of those tasks, without having to involve a secondary vendor? Again, we discovered only two.

What about duopolies? Three stations in the same facility, one with locally programmed music, one with a combination of network and local news/talk, a third with satellite-delivered music? How many suppliers did we find that could handle the entire operation: music, network switching, commercial storage, live assist and fully automated? An exhaustive, two-day search turned up just one.

Dozens of suppliers, hundreds of glossy ads and brochures, thousands of potential sales opportunities all boiled down to finding one supplier who could handle our particular needs. Why?

Many Radio operators have caught a glimpse of the future and can't turn back. Suppliers are scrambling to catch up, but they're seeing the Radio world in terms of old rules.

In the real world, where people actually make things for a living, computers have been doing awesome, complicated tasks that once were done by human beings. Efficiency has improved. Workers have been retrained. Companies have remade themselves, survived and prospered.

Where's The Revolution?

In the Radio business, a seemingly high-tech industry, we transmit signals in the same manner as 80 years ago. We use expensive, unskilled laborers to execute repetitive tasks. We produce our product in virtually the same way today as was done 40 years ago.

If any of us saw a manufacturer operating with 80-year-old technology, we would send him direct to Tom Peters for therapy. But, that's exactly what our industry is: an old, antiquated delivery system utilizing old, antiquated manufacturing techniques.

The manufacturing revolution that has circled the globe cannot bypass our industry. Like the automotive industry or the steel industry, the Radio industry will be re-created. Our delivery system will be reborn. Our manufacturing techniques will be revolutionized. Our workforce will be retrained.

There is a better solution coming, and it will likely be invented by someone from outside our little Radio community. That's bad news for the suppliers at the NAB Radio Show, but very good news for those of us who intend to remain in business long after the position of "disc jockey" has been retired to the Radio Hall of Fame.

Chapter 67

Community-Minded Managers

Involvement Brings Respect, Ratings And Revenue

By Jack M. Rattigan

- When a station is community-minded, organizations come forth with ideas.
- Successful community projects prove Radio works.

Any station worth its license keeps in touch with the community. Everyone should be involved in what's going on in the neighborhood. The GM who attends the children's PTA meeting learns firsthand the challenges that face education today. The sales manager who serves on the fund drive committee for the new wing at the hospital gets to know the cost of medical care today. The program director who listens to the Jaycees' proposal for "on air" help for their latest project learns that people really care. Through this involvement the station can move on to a more realistic approach to serving its audience.

Once your station has a reputation for being community-minded, organizations will start coming to you with ideas and projects. With a little imagination and planning, most of these ideas can be adapted to your station's image and promotion schedule.

Working with the PTA, the hospital building drive or the Jaycees has many benefits. When you are associated with respected charitable institutions, you get volunteers who will do a lot of the "legwork" for you. Those volunteers have business contacts and other connections that you have been trying to get for years. Once you work on these worthwhile projects, you will find a greater respect for your station in the business community. That department store or automobile dealer who would not talk to your sales staff may now welcome them. Through these contacts, you also get cross-promotion through news stories in newspapers and on local TV. The project becomes a true service to the area. There is a variety of good publicity you would never get if it were just a station promotion.

As the promotion progresses, you will once again realize how powerful an instrument Radio can be. Once you comprehend the reaction to the station's accomplishments in gathering crowds, raising money or whatever the goal may be, it will be apparent that Radio works.

While broadcasters know they have a responsibility to serve their community, there are rewards that go beyond fulfilling federally regulated obligations. A station that understands the real needs of its community is much better-prepared to present helpful programming and promotions that boost the station's image and increase its audience.

Chapter 68

Smart Spending

Wise Budgeting Can Improve Sound And Reduce Expenses

By William P. Suffa

- **Sound quality is affected by more than the processing chain.**
- **Smart spending can improve quality and sound for reasonable expense.**
- **Put equipment on a replacement cycle to spread the costs over several years.**

Well, it's that time of year again. The colors of autumn will shortly fade to winter, leaving us to dream of green again. Of course! It's budget time.

What with promotions, talent, debt service and so forth, it's often difficult to find money for engineering needs, particularly capital. After all, the physical equipment is essential for station operation, but it is rarely a revenue center. As an engineer, I do not advocate reckless spending but rather a planned replacement cycle and "smart spending."

Here is what I consider smart spending: expenditures that enhance the station's sound (enhancing service) or improve reliability (reducing operating expense). The smartest spending does both.

Out Of Sight, Out Of Mind

There is a natural tendency to concentrate on the "showy" things — studios, remote vans and so forth. The transmitter plant and antenna equipment are often out of sight — and out of mind. That is, until you are off the air. Then costs skyrocket because of the mad rush to make emergency repairs. By making prudent capital expenditures, operating costs can be reduced, downtime can be minimized and better air sound can ensue.

Here are some things to consider: the age, condition and tuning of your antenna system. We are probably all aware of the hoopla about AM antenna bandwidth a few years ago. I know of one station that revamped its antenna and got calls from competitors asking what it had done. The same applies to FM, except that FM bandwidth markedly affects stereo separation as well as audio quality. If your FM antenna has not been swept for frequency response or is more than a few years old, it is a candidate for improvement expenditure. Other antenna factors that may impact your signal include: the effects of tower mounting on FM systems, AM antenna matching networks or ground systems, AM directional antenna tuning and poor performance of high gain FM antennas. You may find that judicious money spent on antenna maintenance or replacement may produce a better effect on the signal than that new audio processor.

STL systems transmit your audio signal from the studio to the transmitter site. If you're still using leased telephone circuits to provide STL service, consider a microwave system to reduce costs and improve quality. If you have a microwave system, how long has it been since the system was tuned and adjusted? Do you have an adequate backup for the system in case of failure? Remember, the FCC now requires type accepted microwave gear with new frequency tolerances. Older gear (more than about 10 years old) is likely not to meet these requirements. Judicious money spent on improving the STL system can markedly improve the sound and reduce audio distortion.

Candidates For Replacement

How old is your transmitting equipment? Is it so old that parts are difficult and expensive to obtain? Twenty-year-old transmitters are good candidates for replacement, especially with new solid-state technology that can reduce your electric bills and improve the on-air sound. Old and deteriorating equipment often results in much higher operating expenses than the relative cost of new capital investment.

With digital technology moving quickly, it is difficult to determine whether the investment made today will still be useful tomorrow. However, a quick cost/benefit calculation may reveal that using digital storage of spots will save considerable money when compared to carts, even if the system becomes outdated in a few years.

If new equipment is purchased, the older equipment can be held as "reserve" or backup. The backup equipment should be tested periodically to be sure it works when needed.

Finally, if there is some inherent reliability problem at the transmitter or studio site, it may be worth some capital to provide redundancy. An example: WCBS-TV, New York, maintained a fully redundant site at the Empire State Building, allowing it to be the only major New York station to continue operations during the World Trade Center bombing.

With a creative engineering team, reliability can be achieved for relatively small amounts of capital each year. Start by replacing unreliable gear, and put other equipment on a replacement cycle. Without keeping up the transmitting point, you may well find the ratings falling with the autumn leaves next year.

Chapter 69

What Price Does Radio Pay
For Selling Cost Per Point?

By Reed Bunzel

Mark Twain once observed that while everyone talks about the weather, no one ever does anything about it. In Radio, the same thing could be said about cost per point: Everyone talks circles around it, but no one has come up with a more effective alternative to negotiate and sell Radio.

- **Despite complaints, cost per point remains entrenched in the buying and selling of Radio.**
- **Proponents of CPP say it is the most effective means of pricing Radio. The problem, some say, is when broadcasters price their product too low.**
- **CPP's detractors say the method ignores Radio's greatest benefit — the qualitative values of reach, frequency and results.**
- **While the debate will continue, some observers say broadcasters should devote less energy to "bickering" about CPP and more to building opportunities for Radio.**

The battle cries are familiar and plentiful. "As an industry we need to move away from cost per point," the dialogue goes. "Cost per point is a television term, and it only cheapens Radio by driving down market rates. We need to use more qualitative information — and educate the media buyers about effective reach and frequency. If we can only prove that smart use of Radio can yield results, we can crack the system."

Yet, for all the theorizing about alternatives, cost per point remains entrenched in the buying and selling of Radio. Agencies still develop their market cost-per-point analyses, stations still depress their rates to get a piece of the buy and managers curse the day the industry ever accepted "selling by the numbers."

Despite all its deep-rooted — and possibly justifiable — criticism, however, cost per point is not everyone's whipping boy. In fact, while a frustrated and vocal faction curses the day they ever heard the acronym CPP, many others recognize it as a viable tool that serves as a necessary starting block in the negotiating process. As one broadcaster who sees both sides of the question told *Radio Ink*: "We shouldn't all take aim and fire at cost per point, nor should we goose-step to its beat."

The Price Is Right

"We must have some way to determine the price of a station, and I have yet to see a better way of valuing each station than cost per point," says Roy Shapiro, VP/GM at KYW-AM, Philadelphia.

Advertisers, just as all consumers, need to understand the intrinsic value of what they're buying, Shapiro says. "Why is it OK for a client to be told how much an ad will cost them on television, but not on Radio?" he asks. "Cost per point is like the lire in Italy, or the pound in Great Britain — it's Radio's currency."

Bill Burton, president of the Detroit Radio Advertising Group, similarly is critical of broadcasters who "moan about cost per point." A self-declared career salesperson who claims he never has sold strictly by the numbers, Burton firmly believes that "there's really nothing wrong with cost per point; it doesn't prohibit anyone from selling the qualitative aspects of his or her station."

Burton claims that the real problem with cost per point lies with broadcasters who "have no belief in their product — and therefore don't know how to price it." General managers and salespeople who are getting less than market cost per point "perhaps don't have as much to sell, or perhaps they're not selling it as well as other broadcasters," he says. "If a station gets above the cost per point, other stations start complaining that it hurts the other guy who's getting less. When did Radio suddenly become a medium where people go around with a tin cup, saying 'feed me'?"

Shapiro also doesn't buy the notion that many broadcasters feel cost per point belongs strictly in television. "People get hung up on this idea that not all cost per points in Radio are the same, whereas in television they are virtually identical," he explains. "But television cost per point does differ somewhat, because a news show may be worth more than daytime, or prime time could be higher than early fringe. In Radio, the difference in cost per point is determined primarily by format and the kind of listening that accompanies that format." Shapiro notes that such foreground stations as news/talk usually command a higher cost per point because of their commercial environment. "The advertiser pays what he pays because he values the listening environment or the type of person who listens to that station," Shapiro says. "He simply is willing to pay more for that set of ears."

"Cost per point is a terribly misunderstood tool," says Ralph Guild, chairman of Interep. "It is a tool that buyers use to start the negotiating process, and if sellers either overreact to it or take it as gospel, they run the risk of bringing in their stations at a price far lower than anyone ever expected them to." Guild notes that media buyers do not expect all stations in a market to be priced equally, and thus "the cost-per-point spectrum can spread almost 300 percent between the highest and lowest stations in a market."

Thus, stations need to pay attention to how they price themselves. "Many of them have no pricing strategy whatsoever," says Guild. "As a result, every pricing decision seems to be based on who the buyer calls, the mood, time of day and a number of other elements — except true demand." The result: Many stations accept the cost-per-point rate and lose the opportunity to sell that same time to another advertiser for more money before the schedule runs, much the same way airlines price seats or hotels price rooms. A number of Radio stations have adopted rudimentary inventory pricing controls that adequately deal with the general principles of supply and demand, but Guild maintains that broadcasters need to "become as concerned with the time element as they are with demand."

Pressure Cooker

The greater the effort with which the Radio industry pressures demand, "the higher the rates and the less critical cost-per-point buying becomes — particularly on the leading Radio stations," observes Katz Radio Group Chairman Gordon Hastings. "Cost per point is a device used by an agency or a buying service to buy the very best possible Radio stations and the very best possible time for the least amount of money. The job of the rep is to sell advertising time for exactly what that time is worth.

"Whenever a buyer and a seller come together, whether it's on a car lot or at a computer store, there is going to be a price tag ... and a negotiation," Hastings continues. While a Lexus and a Toyota contain many of the same parts, demand for one automobile is greater than for the other — and so is the price. In the case of negotiating Radio spot rates, Hastings says, the process works much the same way. "You can sell your station as a brand, establishing a qualitative value for your station that separates it from the pack because of its qualitative values ... and moves you away from the downward pressures of cost per point."

This deflective movement is critical if Radio is not going to be marketed strictly as a commodity, says Radio Advertising Bureau President

Gary Fries. "Cost per point treats Radio as raw grain leaving the field," he says. "It doesn't extol all its virtues, and it totally ignores everything that it can be made into."

Radio's greatest benefit lies in its qualitative value of being able to reach the consumer, while cost per point is only a system of pricing bodies — a system Fries says reflects "only a very small part of the true value of Radio."

Agencies and buying services that treat cost per point as gospel are overlooking Radio's inherent values and benefits, Fries continues. "Cost per point does nothing to address the ability of the commercial to motivate the customer," he explains. "We need to focus on the benefit to advertisers of the commercial schedule versus the features of the audience. We're trying to focus on the qualitative aspect of Radio, educating people in the creative arena so the quality of the advertising improves ... but at present we have found ourselves presenting cost per point because there is nothing else to work with."

Those in the industry who seek the "ultimate mouse trap" that can kill off cost per point have come up against the hard fact that Radio is an intangible medium. With some 10,000 commercial Radio stations coast-to-coast, advertisers and agencies need a standardized system by which they can maximize their buying efficiency while minimizing the effort — and the risk. Qualitative audience data, while valuable in targeting specific stations, dayparts, audience segments and lifestyle groups, is "difficult to put into a computer, massage and come out with any definitive accuracy," Fries says.

"We've been telling buyers to change, but we haven't given them any alternatives," Fries continues. "If we put ourselves in their shoes, we know that they can't just make decisions without any foundation. They're spending someone else's money, and they can't listen to every salesperson who says 'give me your money, I have a great sales solution to your problem.' "

Quantity Or Quality?

Much of the frustration expressed by station management stems from the often arbitrary calculation by media buyers of market cost per point. "Buyers are always telling us the cost per point for our markets, but in reality we should be setting the cost per point, not the agencies," says Don Kidwell, COO of US Radio. "Our philosophy is 'just say no to low rates,' to educate our people that they don't have to cave in to agency pressure. We need to continue to present qualitative information to advertisers — and then show results."

Essentially, advertisers don't really care about numbers of ratings points or ears; they're trying to move product. "They're looking to see how many cars they can drive off the lot over the weekend, or how many baskets of groceries can be pushed out of the store over the weekend," Kidwell says. "Cost per points doesn't do any of that. What we have to become is much more results-oriented in selling the benefits of what we have to offer."

This marriage of qualitative data and positive results involves positioning, pre-selling and establishing value, says Katz's Gordon Hastings. "We must do those three things. The wheel doesn't need to be reinvented; instead, we need to place more demand against the existing Radio inventory — and we have to qualitatively establish the value of our stations. This is the best way the cost-per-point buying concept can be dealt with."

Part of the persistent cost-per-point problem is that, for every station that fights to get more than its fair share, another station will be willing to eat the market's table scraps. "Some sales managers will always come in over the market cost per point, while others are so desperate to get on the buy that they virtually would drop their drawers," says Coleman Research's Pierre Bouvard, co-developer of Optimum Effective Scheduling. To average out the market cost per point, the higher-priced stations tell the agency "buy us and Mr. Drop-His-Drawers" — and they do it, he says. "These stations figure they're being smart, Mr. Drawers doesn't realize he's being used by his competition and the entire process creates an environment that is detrimental to Radio," Bouvard says.

Equally detrimental are managers who think they're getting above cost per point when, in reality, they're low-balling, Bouvard continues. "Some guy who thinks he's tough will stick to his rate, but then he throws in a bunch of freebies. In his mind he thinks he's holding his rate, but the reality is that if he averages the buy, he's coming in low."

Another reality lies in the fact that, just as all cost per points are not equal, neither are audiences. If three stations each have a 10 share in the prime 25-54 target demo, agencies easily could be misled by buying each station equally. "If three stations are tied 25-54, it would be easy to think they were worth exactly the same," says Rick Pfeiffer, sales manager at WOFM-FM, Wausau, Wisconsin. "But if 85 percent of Station A's listeners are in that 25-54 segment, while only 50 percent of the other station's are 25-54, the buying impact of Station A's listeners is greater." Pfeiffer's point: Cost per point is simply an ersatz formula used by media buyers to justify what they have done, "but because it deals in averages, it doesn't tell you a lot."

Nor does the concept of gross rating point (GRP), which is tangential to selling by cost per point. "Agencies buy gross rating points, but GRP is not something that exists in reality," Pfeiffer says. "It's a mathematical extrapolation." For instance, if an agency wants to deliver 100 rating points — which theoretically is reaching everyone in the target — the agency could reach 25 percent of the people with four times the impact, or it could reach 100 percent of the people one time.

This method of buying time can work effectively on television because viewers tend to choose specific programs, but Radio listeners tend to listen according to station or format — and for considerable lengths of time. For this reason alone, Radio's strengths lie in reach and frequency; therefore, it becomes virtually impossible to determine just how many listeners were reached how many times. "How you arrive at those rating points can be totally disparate and can produce totally different impacts," Pfeiffer says.

Ultimately, the Radio industry will remain split on the merits of cost per point. In one corner, proponents supporting KYW's Roy Shapiro will urge broadcasters to move beyond petty arguments and accept cost per point "so we can sell the effectiveness of this great medium ... and recognize that cost per point is the only way to do it." In the other corner will remain those who believe, as RAB's Gary Fries does, that cost per point ignores reach, frequency and, all too often, results. "Advertisers are becoming results-oriented, and we have to become results-oriented," he cautions.

In any event, laments DRAG's Bill Burton: "Radio people yell and scream too much about cost per point, and we spend too much time, effort and energy in this industry throwing spears at each other." Instead of continuing this bickering, he says, "let's redirect all that energy into building bigger opportunities for the industry ... and increasing Radio's share of the revenue pie."

Chapter 70

OES:
One Step Beyond CPP?

By Reed Bunzel

Originally touted as an effective tool in selling reach and frequency, Optimum Effective Scheduling also has been viewed — and used — by many broadcasters as a way to circumvent much of the frustration of cost per point. While not necessarily developed to bypass CPP numbers-crunching (indeed, OES crunches significant quantities of numbers itself), OES allows Radio salespeople and managers to sell results rather than gross rating points.

By concentrating a greater number of commercials over a shorter period of time than typically are bought in Radio, OES has proved to generate significant increases in in-store traffic, product sales and satisfaction among clients. Extensive research shows that, with the proper product, message and scheduling, an OES package clearly can produce significant results.

What Price Results?

"Cost per point is a pricing tool, and OES is a results tool," observes Coleman Research's Pierre Bouvard, attributing this sage wisdom to Jim Loftus, GM at WARM-AM/WMGS-FM, Wilkes-Barre, Pennsylvania. According to Bouvard, who (with Steve Marx) literally co-wrote the book on OES (*Radio Advertising's Missing Ingredient: The Optimum Effective Scheduling System*, © NAB 1990): "OES is a system that has been documented time and again to blow the doors off results, while CPP is simply a mathematical manipulation that looks at cost and what you're getting. Ultimately, results and pricing are really two different issues."

In fact, OES doesn't necessarily eliminate CPP; it simply focuses the agency less on what Bouvard calls "price nitpicking" and more on asking the question: "How is this going to work for us?" Bouvard admits that the buyer is not going to cave in on CPP without a fight, because buyers generally don't care about results. "They're there to get the job done, to clear the markets," he says. "It's the account executive who cares, because he or she is sweating the renewal. The problem is that a lot of stations try to sell OES when the buy is coming down, and that's the wrong time to do it. They're talking to the wrong person. OES has to be presented in a pre-sell to someone in the agency who cares about results."

Says Interep's Ralph Guild: "OES is absolutely brilliant because it tries to explain mathematically what really works. Any local salesperson knows that you have to run 40-50 spots a week if you're going to get results." Guild concedes that, by targeting just a few stations rather than taking a broad aim at a market, some clients will get more business, while others will be left out of some buys. But, on a national level, "OES doesn't require putting a greater number of spots into a single market. The cost would not necessarily be greater; in fact, it could be lower as you buy more volume on a single station."

"OES relies on saturation, something that virtually has been forgotten in advertising," says John Tenaglia, chairman/CEO of TK Communications. "Most advertisers today look at Radio as an institutional medium, as opposed to a must-produce medium, and that's exactly what OES does. It drives home the message that's important to advertisers because it causes the cash register to ring."

Broadcasters who counter that OES is too expensive are missing the whole point, according to Tenaglia. "What is expensive?" he asks. "If you pay to get the best medical care in the world and it doesn't work, that's expensive. But if you pay the same amount and it does work, it's not expensive. That's what advertisers have to learn." Tenaglia says too many broadcasters have gotten too comfortable with the 25-54 demographic, selling six, 12 or 18 spots spread nicely over Wednesday, Thursday and Friday, 6 a.m. to 7 p.m. "Radio has far more potential than that but, unfortunately, we've been relegated to that because of the cost-per-point mentality."

Critics' Choice

Just as with cost per point, however, OES has met with resistance among many broadcasters and advertisers. The criticisms are many, primary among them the notion that OES schedules are too expensive for many clients to buy ... and the advertiser belief that OES is just another ploy developed by Radio stations to get more money out of them. Few critics question the results documented by OES, but short-term results do not necessarily yield continuous long-term success.

"OES works where and when it is appropriate, but it would be wrong to think that the only way Radio should be bought is through OES," says marketing consultant John Fellows, president of Giraffe Marketing in Falmouth, Maine. "There are other ways to get the frequency and effectiveness in scheduling." Fellows has developed a two-level marketing plan that combines long-term fixed position ads designed to build profile, consistency and awareness among advertisers, and periodic sales promotions utilizing short-duration, OES-type vertical schedules.

The argument against such long-term "high-spot" or "fixed-position" ads is that they don't reach as many people and they sacrifice short-term frequency. "But that frequency is there in the long term, based on the fact that you're taking advantage of consumer lifestyle habits." Fellows concedes that long-term fixed positioning will not turn on a faucet of inquiries, but that is not necessarily its intent. "It is not designed for people who are having a big sale this weekend, because for some products it's best to reach them over time," he says.

The Honeymoon Is Over

OES was developed with the sincere intention of generating respect for Radio from advertisers and agencies by producing significant cash register receipts. And, in many respects, that's exactly what it did. But the OES honeymoon is over, and some advertisers are beginning to balk at the basic tenets of the system. "In reality, OES panders to the we'll-test-you-to-see-if-you-work mentality," says Rick Pfeiffer, sales manager at WOFM-FM in Wausau, Wisconsin. "Having a numerical way to gauge what type of schedule will have good impact is fine, but we should not be using OES as a first approach to new clients, or as our best selling idea." Radio still needs to concentrate on long-term, year-long schedules, which are prohibitively expensive under OES terms — and which focus on the fact that today's Radio listeners are not necessarily today's consumers.

"In the average business, only 2 percent to 8 percent of the market for the average product is a short-term 'now' buyer," says Pfeiffer. "Far more people in the market are NOT going to be a client in the next month than are going to be. OES will work in a short-term, event-oriented test kind of situation, but the only thing that will always work is consistency, because you reach those buyers who are going to be buyers over a longer period of time." Pfeiffer characterizes this notion as a target, with today's customers as the bull's eye — and future customers spread throughout the remaining concentric circles. "The center of the target represents those you can reach with the short-term, whiz-bang schedule, but it doesn't reach those who are going to be buying in the next six months to a year," he explains.

In certain circumstances, OES works wonderfully ... "but it is not necessarily the cure-all to everything," according to RAB President Gary Fries. "It's a step in the direction of finding a frequency schedule that gets results for advertisers, but there is no stock formula ... and people who are trying to find one are going to be very frustrated, because they aren't going to find any answers."

Chapter 71

Progress In Training

Managing Change Is The Key

By Jeremy Millar

- **Training staff to handle change is crucial to long-term survival.**
- **Experiential training accelerates the learning curve.**
- **Empowering staff, blurring job boundaries and removing blame are key benefits along the way.**

Today's Radio station is miles away from its predecessor, and it's a sure bet that tomorrow's will be almost unrecognizable. The thing to remember is that change is a process.

Digital technology, satellites, fiber optics, automation, networking, multi-skilling and job sharing are just the tip of the iceberg. Future changes might include on-demand sales spots and point-of-sale data entry. Managers need to train staff to handle these rapid-fire changes. Easier said than done. As Robert Kennedy observed: "Progress is a nice word. But change is its motivator, and change has its enemies."

There will always be those who oppose change, but managing this natural resistance is crucial to making any real progress.

Ready, Fire, Aim

We undertook a program to manage change with one Radio group by putting its staff through special seminars. The company realized that the systems and structures that had served them profitably in the past were the very things that were likely to strangle them in the future.

The CEO held frank and open meetings with senior managers. Plans were then drawn up to start a re-engineering program that became known in-house as "the ready, fire, aim" program, a name that reflected the need to do something quickly.

In face-to-face meetings between staff (who were needed to help management solve its problems) and management, the main objective was communicated: There are plenty of program-oriented Radio businesses and many more sales-focused businesses, but as for customer-obsessed Radio stations — well, that's a different story.

Phase one consisted of five identical training seminars with around 30 staff participating in each. The training program started early on a Friday afternoon and finished on Saturday evening.

The first part of the course was a "state of the industry" discussion, detailing key trends and projections. Then we opened the books and discussed the nuts and bolts of the company's operating plans and objectives.

Next, we divided the staff into groups and gave them three key questions to consider: What business are we in? Who is our customer? How can we better deliver to our customer? Each group reported back, and discussion followed on internal and external customer needs. Later, we viewed a short business video on paradigm shifts, and followed it with further group activity. Then we formed new groups to brainstorm solutions and ideas to meet the needs identified by research.

We finished work around 9 p.m. However, the night didn't end until the early hours, with barroom discussion being an important component of the secondary objective — team building.

Day two moved out of the classroom with the experiential component of the program. Experiential training speeds the learning curve by "doing," namely via short outdoor activities followed by debriefs and group reports. The teams related each of their activities to the workplace, with staff quickly making the crucial links between the exercises and work. This led to a better understanding of workplace dynamics, such as objective setting, trust and support, strategies and decision-making, communication, issues and conflict, leadership and fun.

Empowering Staff

Group notes were summarized and circulated within a week. Follow-up focus groups with ad hoc groupings of staff went on to identify problems and possible solutions, and this led to stage two of the training program: the removal of blame and empowerment of staff.

Proof that empowerment was creeping in was illustrated when a morning jock on one of the company's stations wrote a sales prop for another of the company's stations. He went on to successfully present this to the client, taking an active role in sales, creative and production in the process.

More job boundaries began to blur. Customer focus groups became common, with staff encouraged to participate in the subsequent decision-making and problem-solving. Layers of middle management began downsizing and refocusing.

Stage three's skills audit identified specific training needs. Appropriate training modules helped raise individual skill levels so that all staff could become multitalented and able to present specific skills to their employer.

A program to manage change can be fitted to any business. It could be crucial to your progress.

Chapter 72

Choosing A Tower Crew

Lessons In Self-Protection

By George Whitaker

I have learned a couple of very important lessons about choosing tower companies and dealing with tower crews. Consider the following, which happened to me a number of years ago in Arkansas.

The freight company delivered the tower sections, line, antenna and all necessary hardware. I inspected all the items as they were unloaded and did not find any shipping damage. I signed the receipt and then proceeded to check the packing slips against the order and the actual materials on hand. All necessary materials were there and in good condition.

The tower crew then arrived and proceeded to stack steel. After the tower was up and the antenna mounted, the next step was to install the line. At this point, the tower crew chief came to me and said that the adapter that was to go between the cable and the antenna wasn't there. He suggested that I could order one, but they had another job to get to and couldn't wait. They could come back in a couple of weeks and finish up. However, they had one on the truck that had never been used and I could get the job finished if I bought theirs. I agreed to do so.

Then, when the line was installed on the tower and we were ready to connect to the transmitter, the elbow couldn't be found. However, they had one on the truck, etc. I agreed to buy their elbow.

Won't Get Fooled Again

Having learned a lesson, I adopted the following procedure: I took the crew chief around as soon as the tower crew arrived and checked each packing slip against the materials on hand and checked again for any possible shipping damage. Then, I had him sign each packing slip, with any damage of any kind noted in his writing on the packing slip associated with that particular item. I never had any missing parts after that.

Another thing I have learned is that the cheapest tower company is not always the cheapest in the long run. I have been called in on more than one occasion to try to straighten out a mess created by an incompetent crew.

Before signing the contract, ask for a list of all of the crew's customers for the past 18 months. Call some of them and check to see what kind of problems they have had. Also, ask them if they know any other stations that this tower company has done work for. You may find that there are stations the tower company did not provide on their list. A call to those stations might be much more revealing than the ones the company gave you.

An incompetent or undercapitalized tower company can cost you thousands, even hundreds of thousands. Taking the time and trouble to check references is vital.

Chapter 73

Controlling The Forecast

It All Comes Down To Making The Right Assumptions

By Ellyn F. Ambrose

You're finishing the year 15 percent below forecast and completing next year's plan, and your bank is breathing down your neck for a projection you can make. What do you do?

Broadcasting: The business of producing inventory to sell for a profit. The audience determines the value of that inventory, and we access that audience with programming. The "price" is negotiated and is a function of supply (inventory in the marketplace that is unsold) and demand (the amount of revenue available in the marketplace ... what the advertiser's CPP budget is and what everyone else is charging).

- **Accurate business plans depend on knowledge of the market and its history.**
- **Plan for your share of revenue to be consistent with previous years; base your pricing on demand.**
- **Determine who the pricing leader is in the market, and follow their lead.**
- **Involve your sales staff in the problem-solving process. Give clear goals and objectives; make sure they know how to deal with hidden objections.**

In any manufacturing business, a business plan is only as good as its assumptions. Profitability is not only a function of sales and expenses, but also our ability to perform the "management task," getting maximum performance out of our people to ensure a spectacular operation. Staff productivity combined with effective cost controls and sensational sales yields the greatest cash flow.

So, if you're not making your plan, don't immediately terminate your sales manager; ask yourself critical questions to focus on your business plan assumptions. Answers yield knowledge, which affects our ability to make those critical decisions and assumptions.

Re-evaluate your goals and objectives; review them with your sales manager and program director: What is your market forecast? What share of market revenue do you project? What is your audience goal? What is your sellout percentage? Have you set goals for each salesperson individually? What is your marketing and sales support effort?

Knowledge Plus History

Market Forecast: Track available revenue in your market for the last several years. Determine the average percent of available revenue by month and by quarter. This is an "average monthly demand." Now, compare the monthly and quarterly percents of your revenue to available market revenue. If your business plan calls for 22 percent of your revenue in the first quarter, and the available market revenue is traditionally 20 percent in that period, you have overprojected the first quarter. You would have to raise your pricing significantly to maximize your inventory for the balance of the year, but your CPMs would be higher than the market.

Now you say: "Wait, these are the '90s. The business is changing. How can we use historical perspective to project another questionable year?" The business has changed in that clients tend to hold onto their advertising dollars as long as possible, but both local and national advertising dollars are a function of sales. There is never a black-and-white answer to the question of market forecasting. You must evaluate your market and local employment figures, watch retail sales events and real estate sales, and project based on knowledge plus history. Maybe a Ford Motor Co. plant shut down, eliminating 1,200 jobs. Of course, you wouldn't use an average including revenue historical numbers, although the percentage by quarter should be close.

Also remember that national advertisers don't learn the results of their advertising campaigns until their distribution reports come in, but your local retailer knows the day of the event. Sales success or failure determines what their advertising budget is going to be for the next one.

Share of Revenue: Compare your revenue share for the last several years and this year to date. Is your projected share higher than last year? If your station has never achieved more than a seven share of revenue and your plan calls for a nine, you have to rethink your assumptions. With pricing strategies based on supply and demand, you should plan for your share of revenue to be consistent; your pricing must anticipate demand. For example, never cut the rate in May when you know that you're sold out every year, but do anything you want in January. Or, December is always 75 percent sold out because it's a three-week month — but those first three weeks? Premium plus.

Follow The Leader

Audience: Is your audience comparable to the audience projected in your plan? Is it up or down? (If your audience is up, your revenue should be higher than in your plan.) Are you a Generation X station, missing dollars in the 25-54 demo? Break out your audience and determine the cost per point or CPM that you've historically sold the station for, versus what you're selling it for now. Then, determine the competitive CPMs and CPPs. Teach your salespeople that getting competitive is part of their job; detailed competitive schedules and dollars are absolutely essential for you to read your market and project. What do your clients buy and what do they pay for it? There will always be surprises in competitive information — that "nothing" competitor who consistently gets "love" or "client dictate" buys; that station behind you in audience that's getting a higher average price.

Soon, you'll determine who is the pricing leader in your market. If your audience is at his level, less than or more than, follow his lead.

Here's a classic example (and a true story). Two GMs have both done a spectacular job. The first changed format and took the station to fifth in adults 25-54, cash flow from break even to almost $3 million. A six share of audience; 6 percent of the revenue.

However, the competitor down the street is seventh or eighth in the demographic. With half the audience share (three), he's getting a five share of revenue and cash flowing $3 million. This super sales performer does four things extremely well: He follows the pricing leader, he sells cume, he bonuses retailers so he can ensure results and he packages everything on the Radio station.

Sellout Percentage: What sellout percentage did you estimate in your plan? Supply/demand pricing dictates that you should price yourself to be 95 percent sold out for 12 months per year. In the first-quarter, did you have good rates at a 60 percent sellout? Are you 93 percent sold out at low rates and off plan? In both cases, you're not priced correctly.

Inventory is perishable; every spot has a value because you spent money to create it. Why not bonus those marginal first-quarter buys to secure every piece of business, use those announcements to make up audience shortfalls from your last book, bonus a retail client to secure the next order at increased rates?

Support Your Staff

Sales Management and Sales Accountability: Have you established clear goals and objectives for your staff by month and by quarter? Do you give them recaps of goals and sales to date? Do you reward them for high performance? Do they make enough calls? Do they notify you of opportunities? What is their closing percentage? The most important thing for the station is sales; the most important thing for a salesperson to do is to close the sale. If you have seemingly experienced salespeople who are not getting orders, you are dealing with hidden objections. They must learn to determine those objections.

Investment in sales training — whether in the form of media sales tapes or hiring a sales consultant — always reaps rewards.

Marketing and Sales Support: Do you market and promote your station to full advantage to generate advertising revenue? Do you promote effectively? Do you provide your salespeople with support to overcome those "hidden objections"? Are you, the GM or owner, willing to maintain relationships with your clients? Do you go to their promotions? Is your on-air staff willing to make appearances? Do you create and maximize PR opportunities? Is your program director creating the "right" promotions to close those 52-week retailers? Do the promotion, sales and programming departments work together as a team?

If you're missing your forecast, you must find out why. You must examine your original assumptions. Market revenue could be off, your price might be too high or too low, you might not be packaging your station competitively or effectively enough, you might have misallocated your monthly forecast, you might simply not be selling enough, your sales manager might not be pulling it together or your salespeople might not be making calls or closing. Ask questions. The answers will define the issues, which is the most difficult part.

With leadership and management, involving your staff in this problem-solving process, they will make up that 15 percent difference. Be involved with them. Define their goals clearly and objectively. Engage them in a participatory way; you'll be astounded at their solutions.

Chapter 74

Improving Caller Audio

Three Options

By Roy Pressman

Telephone systems have become an integral part of our broadcast operations. Aside from airing telephone conversations with the jock or talk show host, telephone lines are the best way to "hear" what the listeners want.

But putting telephone calls on the air can turn off your listeners if you're not careful. Telephone lines are hardly high fidelity. Add some noise and few percent of distortion and you can end up with a mess.

- **The telephone coupler is a passive device that hooks directly to the telephone line.**
- **A properly utilized speakerphone can sound extremely good on the air.**
- **Digital hybrids can automatically equalize the caller's audio and can adjust the volume of the caller with a compressor/expander.**

Three Ways To Improve Audio

Don't just hook up anything to a telephone line to get caller audio. All connections to the telephone line must be made via FCC-approved equipment. There are three good ways to get caller audio from the telephone: telephone coupler, speakerphone, digital hybrid system.

Telephone coupler: The telephone coupler is a passive device that hooks directly to the telephone line. Various manufacturers make these couplers, and they connect easily to the studio mixing console.

Positives: Inexpensive, typically between $50 and $200; easy to hook up.

Negatives: The output has a mix of both the caller audio and the air personality's audio, but the caller's audio is much lower in volume. Stations typically boost the caller's audio to the correct level, but this makes the jock's level too high and sounds extremely distorted. So, the coupler is not really suited for on-air conversations. They should only be used to feed audio down the telephone line or to record audio from the telephone line.

Speakerphone: A properly utilized speakerphone can sound extremely good on the air. Since most Radio studios are equipped with speakerphones, there is usually little or no investment. A tap can connect the speakerphone speaker to the mixing console. This allows the jock to speak to the caller on the air without level/distortion problems. Sometimes a compressor/expander can tailor the speakerphone sound.

Positives: Audio output is easily obtained from the speakerphone speaker; audio output contains only the caller's audio.

Negatives: Speakerphones are switching-type devices — only one person can speak at a time (the caller or the on-air personality), and the volume control on the speakerphone can be set too high, causing the caller's audio to be extremely distorted. Some speakerphones do not have good audio quality at any listening level.

Digital hybrid: To enable us to simultaneously talk and listen from a single pair of wires (a standard telephone line), we need to use a device called a hybrid. All telephone sets contain hybrids. The hybrid converts the incoming two-wire telephone line to four wires — two for send (connected to the mouthpiece) and two for receive (connected to the earpiece or receiver). Telephone hybrids have a certain amount of leakage. Some of what we're sending gets into the receive side. It's no big deal; in fact the leakage is the reason you can hear yourself on the telephone earpiece when you speak into the telephone mouthpiece.

More From The Hybrid

For Radio and on-air use, we need to ask a lot more from the hybrid. Although analog hybrid systems are available, a few manufacturers, Telos and Gentner specifically, have come up with digital hybrid systems that address most of the problems of interfacing the studio with the telephone system. These digital hybrids compensate for differing phone lines, which minimizes hybrid leakage. They can automatically equalize the caller's audio and can adjust the volume of the caller with a compressor/expander. If your studio is equipped with the standard 1A2 10-button telephone set, interfacing with any one of the new digital hybrids is a snap. But interfacing can be achieved with other phone systems, as well.

Positives: The caller and jock can talk simultaneously without distortion, automatic adjustment to different telephone lines, automatic gain adjustment of caller audio, ability to send pre-delay audio to caller (if your program is on delay) and the ability to send any audio to the caller (such as mix-minus).

Negatives: Systems can be expensive ($800-$4,000). If the hybrid cannot properly adjust to the selected telephone line, leakage can cause the announcer's audio to sound hollow or tinny.

Listen, then talk to your engineer and discuss ways to improve your system.

Chapter 75

The Manager As Referee

In A Station's Family Feud

By Jack M. Rattigan

- in-house wars are destructive and counterproductive.
- A manager cannot take sides in departmental feuds, and must be fair and stern at the same time.
- Every staff member must understand and appreciate everyone else's role.

The more Radio people I speak with, the more I realize that so many stations are still having a "family feud." Stations are on the street every day telling agencies and retailers not to advertise on other stations. RAB, state associations and city organizations are working very hard to crush this practice.

Even more destructive and perplexing are the in-house wars, which usually involve sales vs. programming; with LMAs and duopolies, the problem may be even greater. Staffs that a few weeks ago were archenemies must now blend into one organization. How do we stop this infighting? The task falls on the shoulders of the manager because the manager is responsible for the vitality of the entire organization.

There are some "basics" managers have a responsibility to convey to their staffs. They must instill in their people the idea that sales and programming are equally accountable for success of the station(s). It helps if the program director attends sales meetings on a regular schedule and the sales manager attends program meetings.

Management must constantly point out successes of programming to the sales department, and vice versa. Where LMAs and/or duopolies are involved, the manager has to fashion a plan so that everyone understands the role of each station and why each station has its own value and goals.

Pride Or Poor Management?

Why, then, is there discord? Some call it pride. Some call it competitiveness. I call it "poor management." How can we serve our listeners and our clients when we are too busy serving our self-interests? Why not spend more time and effort creating a cohesive and harmonious team so that we can have a more efficient and productive staff? None of this can happen if our department heads are resentful of each other. Teamwork and cooperation are essential ingredients in a profitable operation.

When conflict results, management cannot take sides. Like a good parent, the manager must respect everyone with equality, and be fair and stern at the same time. A successful station must strive to be like the perfect family. A superstar manager has to be a guardian, a respected leader, a trendsetter ... and a diplomat.

Does it work? You bet. I have been fortunate to have been part of such operations (successful operations) where the sales manager respected the program director. She appreciated the good programming that made the station easier to sell. The PD realized that the sales staff was "bringing in the bucks" that made it possible to attract and keep outstanding talent and put together exceptional promotions. And each station celebrated the success of its "sister station."

Chapter 76

Buyer Beware

Pre-Purchase Station Inspection Can Save You Thousands

By William F. Suffa

It never ceases to amaze me that station purchasers will perform extensive due diligence on the financial and programming operations of a prospective station but ignore the technical side. With duopoly and the renewal of the buy-sell-trade market for broadcast facilities, there are bargains to be had. There are also real risks for purchasers, which could leave sellers laughing all the way to the bank.

- **A technical due diligence inspection is like a pre-purchase home inspection to evaluate the condition and operation of station equipment.**
- **Technical due diligence can save a lot of money and aggravation for purchasers.**
- **Buyers should avoid requests to conduct inspections in secrecy. This can hide problems that would otherwise be uncovered by speaking with the current engineering staff.**

Consider, if you will, the results of this nation's fine economic performance over the past few years, the amount of debt service paid by stations during that time and the lack of capital expenditure that resulted. Consider that station budgets were slashed, reducing staff and maintenance to a minimum. Consider that many stations were shoehorned into existence and probably should never have been built. Consider whether the seller is willing to warrant that the station really can be upgraded.

A Pre-Purchase Inspection

Before jumping off the roof or calling off that purchase deal, there is some wisdom to performing due diligence on the technical installation and potential for your new purchase. For a modest cost, relative to the purchase price, you can have an engineering evaluation done of the technical facilities. Think of it like a "pre-purchase home inspection" for Radio facilities.

A typical due diligence inspection will evaluate the condition and operation of your prospective purchase to identify: the condition and age of equipment, impending capital purchase requirements, operational difficulties, recommended improvements, compliance with FCC regulations, a search of FCC records, defects in the station coverage and audio.

Optionally, buyers can obtain evaluations of upgrade potential, staff performance, prospective areas for reducing budget, operational layout, full inventory check, RF energy exposure (environmental) and other matters of interest.

Selecting a competent inspector and setting parameters on the inspection can be difficult. Most good consulting practices offer a range of services and experience to perform such an inspection. You'll want to avoid: contractors who are on the take from equipment vendors, "engineers" who lack adequate background or experience and engineers who will not work with you to define the scope of the inspection. Remember, the inspection report will form a basis of negotiation for concessions (or escrows) in the purchase contract, so the integrity and writing ability of the engineer/inspector is paramount.

An Expense That Saves

Each client and station is different. Some insist on detailed, careful counts of each screw and nut; others just seek an overview of the situation to avoid unpleasant surprises (banks and investors usually insist on the greatest detail). Similarly, most evaluations can be made with the station on the air and off the air (particularly if an unsatisfactory condition is identified). Since consultants charge on an hourly/daily basis, a clear scope of work should be defined before the inspection takes place. Typical inspection costs will range from $2,000 to $7,500 per station, depending on the detail requested.

Remember, the inspection is a snapshot of the station as it exists when the inspection takes place; there are no guarantees that the station will be 100 percent trouble-free at closing.

One more thing: Often a buyer makes a request to have the station inspected in "secrecy." Not a good idea, since most often the station staff knows of an impending sale anyway, and the station engineer can add great perspective to the inspection, which often results in a better analysis.

I still remember someone who failed to have an inspection done and ended up spending, literally, hundreds of thousands of dollars on rebuilding and adjusting an AM directional antenna (and, after all that, still ended up reducing power by 50 percent to meet FCC restrictions).

By contrast, another potential purchaser walked away from a deal based on an unsatisfactory inspection report. The $3,000 inspection expense saved more than $100,000 in repairs (for a $500,000 purchase deal).

Caveat emptor.

AMBROSE, ELLYN F. is CEO of The Marketing Group Inc. in Washington, D.C. She may be reached at 703-903-9500.

ANTHONY, DAVE is president of Anthony Media Concepts, a broadcast consulting company. He may be reached at 904-693-5235.

BACHMAN, KATY is a free-lance writer and editor. She may be reached at 203-353-8717.

BADER, MICHAEL H. is at the law firm of Haley, Bader & Potts. He may be reached at 703-841-0606.

BERG, MICHAEL is an attorney in Washington, D.C.

BERKOWITZ, CLIFF is president of Paradigm Radio, a Radio promotions and marketing consulting firm. He may be reached at 707-443-9842.

BOLTON, TED is president of Philadelphia-based Bolton Research Corp., a Radio research and marketing firm, and publisher of Radio Trends. He may be reached at 610-640-4400.

BOSLEY, RHODY is a partner with Research Director, Inc., a sales and marketing consultancy based in Baltimore. He may be reached at 410-377-5859.

BOYD, CLIFF is the president of Cash Flow Management. He has an extensive and diverse background in public and private financing and is passionately committed to providing the financial planning and partnerships necessary to allow all-size Radio stations to grow and prosper. He may be reached at 214-780-0081.

BROWN, LINDA G. may be reached through Eagle Marketing Services, Inc. at 303-484-4736.

BUNZEL, REED is vice president/communications at the Radio Advertising Bureau. He previously held the position of executive editor of Radio Ink, and has served in editorial capacities at Broadcasting magazine, Radio and Records and the National Association of Broadcasters. Bunzel is the author of "Pay For Play," a mystery novel published by Avon Books.

BIOGRAPHIES:

BURTON, BILL is president and COO of the Detroit Radio Advertising Group. He travels around the country touting his trademark and signature, "Be Fabulous," and is known for his crazy "stunts" and attention-getting ways. Burton holds a degree in business and economics from Michigan State University. He may be reached at 810-643-7455.

CARLOUGH, JUDY is the executive vice president of the Radio Advertising Bureau's national marketing efforts. She has more than 16 years experience in Radio sales and management at ABC RADIO, INFINITY BROADCASTING and NOBLE BROADCASTING, and for several years was an on-air personality in Boston. Prior to joining the RAB, she was the vice president and general manager of XTRA-AM. She may be reached at 212-387-2100.

CASE, DWIGHT is currently the president of Motivational Incentives Group and a member of WIMC's Executive Committee. He presently owns KOQO AM & FM and KSQR AM & FM, and has a 35-year history in broadcasting. His journalism experience includes four years as the publisher and chief executive of Radio & Records. He may be reached at 310-854-7505.

CHAPIN, RICHARD W. holds the distinction of being the only person ever to be elected as chairman of both the Radio Advertising Bureau and the National Association of Broadcasters. He has been recognized as R.C. Crisler & Company's leading volume broker, and has received numerous broadcasting awards and citations throughout the years.

CIMBERG, ALAN is a noted sales motivational speaker and trainer. He may be reached at 516-593-7099.

COLOMBO, GEORGE is a nationally recognized speaker and writer on sales and management topics. He is a regular columnist for Selling magazine and the author of the McGraw-Hill best seller "Sales Force Automation." Colombo has shared his message with thousands of sales professionals in workshops and presentations nationwide. He may be reached at 407-327-2453.

COOKE, HOLLAND is a Washington, D.C.-based programming consultant specializing in news/talk and full-service AM. He may be reached at 202-333-8442.

CORNILS, WAYNE is a vice president at the Radio Advertising

Bureau. He may be reached at 212-254-2142.

CRAIN, DR. SHARON is a leading industrial psychologist, educator and author. Her client list includes National Association of Broadcasters, USA Today, American Association of Advertising Agencies and Radio Advertising Bureau. Crain has appeared on The Today Show, Good Morning America and many others. She may be reached at 602-483-2546.

DONALDSON, MIMI is an experienced management consultant, trainer and speaker. She spent 10 years as a staff trainer in Human Resources at Walt Disney Productions, Northrop Aircraft and Rockwell International, and has been president of her own consulting company for the past 10 years. She may be reached at 310-273-2633.

FELLOWS, JOHN, CRMC, Mr. Radio™, is highly regarded as an author, speaker and sales professional. His practical sales and advertiser workshops have proven beneficial for associations, groups and stations. His latest book and workshop, "How To Get Rewarding Results With Radio Advertising," is now available. He may be reached at 800-587-5756.

FISHER, GARY is currently vice president and general manager at SW Radio Networks. Previously, he was the vice president and general manager at WNIC/WMTG Detroit and WHTZ New York, and the vice president and general sales manager at WABC MusicRadio/TalkRadio New York. He may be reached at 212-445-5409.

FRIEDMAN, NANCY, the Telephone "Doctor"®, is recognized as "America's formost and most sought-after speaker on customer service and telephone skills." She has spoken before many of the most prestigious associations and organizations around the world, and has appeared on many leading Radio and television programs. She also has a best-selling video and audio training library currently available in eight languages. She may be reached at 800-882-9911.

GABLE, CHRIS of Chris Gable Broadcast Services, a national Radio consulting firm, offers support for programming, management, marketing and development. He may be reached at 717-964-3255.

GALLAGHER, ANN may be reached at 202-619-2189.

GALLAGHER, GINA may be reached at 414-272-6119.

BIOGRAPHIES:

GIFFORD, DAVE is a sales and management consultant from Santa Fe, New Mexico. He may be reached at 1-800-TALK-GIF.

GOULD, MARTY may be reached at 419-228-9248.

HERWEG, ASHLEY and GODFREY are international seminar leaders who have owned, operated and managed stations in small, medium and large markets. They have also co-authored the informative "MAKING MORE MONEY ... Selling Radio Advertising Without Numbers" and "Recruiting, Interviewing, Hiring and Developing Superior Salespeople." Both may be reached at 803-559-9603.

HESSER, MICHAEL B. may be reached at 805-543-9214.

HOFBERG, BUNNY may be reached at 212-613-3816.

KARL, E. is president of E. Karl Broadcast Consulting, a Radio programming and marketing firm. He may be reached at 805-927-1010.

KEITH, MICHAEL C. is a member of the communications department at Boston College. He has also held various positions at several Radio stations and served as the Chair of Education for the Museum of Broadcast Communications. Additionally, he is the author of several books on electronic media, including "Signals On The Air," "The Radio Station" and The Broadcast Century." He may be reached at 617-552-8837.

KNOX, BRIAN K. may be reached through Interep at 212-818-8933.

LeNOBLE, DR. PHILIP J. is chairman of Executive Decision Systems Inc., a human resource, sales training and personal development company in Littleton, Colorado. He may be reached at 303-795-9090.

LONTOS, PAM, president of Lontos Sales & Motivation Inc., customizes seminars, keynotes and "in-station" consulting for stations or associations. She may be reached at 714-831-8861.

LUND, JOHN is president of Lund Media Research and The Lund Consultants to Broadcast Management, Inc., a full-service Radio research, programming and consulting firm dedicated to assisting Radio stations achieve better programming, higher ratings, greater revenue and increased profitability. He may be reached at 415-692-7777.

LYTLE, CHRIS, president of The AdVisory Board Inc., is author of the Radio Marketing Master Diploma Course. He may be reached at 800-255-9853.

MAGUIRE, KATHRYN is president of Revenue Development Systems. She may be reached at 617-589-0695.

MAKI, VAL serves as vice president/general sales manager for WKQX-FM Chicago and has been involved with sales development for Chicago's EMMIS Broadcasting for the past 10 years. She may be reached at 312-527-8348.

MARTIN, ANDREA may be reached at 206-443-9400.

McDANIEL, MIKE, producer of the Action Auction promotion nationwide, has written a book about promotions, and owns and operates two Radio stations. He may be faxed at 812-847-0167.

OTT, RICK is president of the management consulting firm Ott & Associates in Richmond, Virginia, and author of "Unleashing Productivity!" and "Creating Demand." He may be reached at 804-276-7202.

PRESSMAN, ROY is director of engineering for WLVE/WINZ/WZTA in Miami. He may be reached at 305-654-9494.

RATTIGAN, JACK M., CRMC, is president of Rattigan Radio Services, a management and sales consulting company headquartered in Portsmouth, Virginia. He conducts his "The Basics & Beyond" one-day seminars in various markets. Previously, he worked in Philadelphia for NBC, Group W and Metro Media. He may be reached at 804-484-3017.

SABO, WALTER is president of Sabo Media, a management consulting firm based in New York, specializing in turnaround strategies for major market stations. He may be reached at 212-808-3005.

SISLEN, CHARLES may be reached at 212-424-6417.

SKIDELSKY, BARRY is an attorney and consultant, concentrating his efforts in the Radio industry. A frequent author and speaker, he is licensed to practice law in New York and Washington. His background includes 15 years in Radio programming, sales and management. He may be reached at 212-832-4800.

BIOGRAPHIES:

SUFFA, WILLIAM P., P.E. is vice president and management principal of Suffa & Cavell, Inc., with 18 years of experience in Radio communications systems engineering to his credit. As a private consultant, he has provided services for more than 450 clients in the telecommunications and broadcasting fields. Suffa is an author of a monthly column in Radio Ink. He may be reached at 703-591-0110.

TROUT, JACK is president of Trout & Ries marketing strategists in Greenwich, Connecticut. He may be reached at 203-622-4312.

WHITAKER, GEORGE is the author and publisher of Practical Radio Communications, a monthly newsletter that teaches Radio engineering to beginners. He has served as chief engineer for KRVA-AM/FM, Dallas, and is author of the book "Radio Engineering for the Non-Engineer: What Managers Need to Know About Engineering." He may be reached at 800-572-8394.

ZAPOLEON, GUY is president of Zapoleon Media Strategies and works with associates Jeff Scott and Steve Wyrostok. He may be reached at 713-980-3665.

MANAGEMENT AND SALES MANAGEMENT INDEX

A

B

C

D

RADIO INK BACK ISSUES AVAILABLE!

The issues of *Radio Ink* that you've missed are now available in limited supply. Hundreds of moneymaking ideas, interviews, sales tips, copy ideas, packages, marketing strategies and more that you can use now!

VISA, MASTERCARD and AMERICAN EXPRESS accepted!

Normally $4.50 each!
1 to 3 issues $4 each ($2.50 S&H)
4 to 6 issues $3.50 each ($3.50 S&H)
7 to 10 issues $3 each ($4.50 S&H)
11 or more $2.50 each ($6.50 S&H)
(Florida residents add 6% sales tax.)

#1 Jan. 8, '90
Cover: The Future Of Radio - A Look At The Decade Ahead
Interview: Dick Harris

#2 Jan. 15, '90
Cover: What The RAB Can Do For You:
Interview: Robert Sillerman

#3 Jan. 22, '90
Cover: Radio Commercials On TV
Interview: Carl Wagner

#4 Jan. 29, '90
Cover: An Arbitron Radio Diary
Interview: Jerry Cliffton

#5 Feb. 5, '90
Cover: Radio Group Heads (What They Look For When Hiring A GM)
Interview: Frank Wood

#6 Feb. 12, '90
Cover: Taking Over As GM
Interview: Ken Swetz

#7 Feb. 19, '90
Cover: Strange Bedfellows? (When Radio Owners Own Another Business)
Interview: Bob Fuller

#8 Feb. 26, '90
Cover: Pork Rinds And Porsches (Country Radio Goes To Town)
Interview: Bob Meyer

#9 Mar. 5, '90
Cover: Doing Remotes Fron Fantasyland (What Disney Has To Offer)
Interview: Steve Berger

#10 Mar. 12, '90
Cover: We Can Help (Executive Search Firms Answer Radio's Questions)
Interview: Aaron Daniels

#11 Mar. 26, '90
Cover: Hiring Sales Superstars
Interview: Carl E. Hirsch

#12 Apr. 9, '90
Cover: Employer Expectations And Employee Rights (How Much Should Be In Writing)
Interview: Marc Guild

#13 Apr. 16, '90
Cover: Power Collections
Interview: Ted & Todd Hepburn

#14 Apr. 23, '90
Cover: Training Radio Superstar Salespeople
Interview: Art Carlson

#15 Apr. 30, '90
Cover: Could Cable Sales Hurt Radio?
Interview: Tom Gammon

#16 May 14, '90
Cover: Researching The Researchers
Interview: Scott Ginsburg

#17 May 21, '90
Cover: Buying Your First Station: A Primer
Interview: Alan Box

#18 Jun. 4, '90
Cover: Rise Reported in Listening Levels
Interview: Al Sikes

#19 Jun. 11, '90
Cover: Hiring A PD
Interview: Jerry Lyman

#20 Jun. 18, '90
Cover: Back To School
Interview: Robert Kipperman

#21 Jul. 2, '90
Cover: EZ Listening: Eye of the Storm
Interview: Herb McCord

#22 Jul. 9, '90
Cover: A Look At The Direct Mail, Telemarketing for Radio
Interview: Raul Alarcon

#23 Jul. 16, '90
Cover: National Business
Interview: Mike Oatman

#24 Jul. 23, '90
Cover: Handcuffed By Your Sales Image
Interview: Michael J. Faherty

#25 Jul. 30, '90
Cover: New Life For News/Talk
Interview: Randy Michaels

#26 Aug. 6, '90
Cover: Traffic And Billing Systems
Interview: Jim Duncan

#27 Aug. 13, '90
Cover: Marketing Your Radio Station (How to Formulate A Strategic Plan)
Interview: Les Goldberg

#28 Aug. 20, '90
Cover: Effective Budgeting
Interview: Ted Nixon

TO ORDER BACK ISSUES: CALL 1-800-226-7857

#29 Aug. 27, '90
Cover: Twenty-Four Hour Syndicated Programming
Interview: Jay Cook

#30 Sep. 3, '90
Cover: New Technology For Radio
Interview: Alexander Williams

#31 Sep. 17, '90
Cover: Goodbye To Boston
Interview: Jim Thompson

#32 Sep. 24, '90
Cover: '90 Marconi Awards
Interview: Bob Hughes

#33 Oct. 1, '90
Cover: Helping Your Clients Develop Marketing Strategies
Interview: Steve Edwards

#34 Oct. 8, '90
Cover: Sales Presentations
Interview: Frank Osborn

#35 Oct. 15, '90
Cover: A Niche In Time
Interview: Dick Ferguson

#36 Oct. 29, '90
Cover: When To Walk
Interview: Nick Verbitsky

#37 Nov. 5, '90
Cover: Correction or Catastrophe: (The Year In Trading)
Interview: Jeffrey E. Trumper

#38 Nov. 12, '90
Cover: Sales and Management Consultants
Interview: Stanley Mak

#39 Nov. 19, '90
Cover: Black-Owned Radio
Interview: Pierre Sutton

#40 Nov. 26, '90
Cover: Back to Basics and Beyond
Interview: Mickey Franko

#41 Dec. 3, '90
Cover: Libraries and Custom Commercials
Interview: Michael Bader

#42 Dec. 10, '90
Cover: Managing A Radio Station In A Recession
Interview: Dan Mason

#43 Jan. 14, '91
Interview: Ralph Guild (Radio Executive of the Year)

#44 Jan. 21, '91
Cover: Making TV Work Harder For Radio
Interview: Rick Buckley

#45 Feb. 4, '91
Cover: Tools That Make Your Station Sound Great
Interview: Rick Dees

#46 Mar. 18, '91
Cover: Hot Sales Prospects
Interview: Mark Hubbard

#47 Apr. 1, '91
Cover: Interactive Phone Systems
Interview: Bill Steding

#48 Apr. 29, '91
Cover: Advice From Great Operators
Interview: Marty Greenberg

#49 May 13, '91
Cover: Selling Car Dealers
Interview: Sally Jessy Raphael

#50 May 27, '91
Cover: Research Strategies
Interview: Terry Jacobs

#51 Jun. 10, '91
Cover: Changing Face Of Radio Engineering
Interview: Dick Kalt

#52 Jul. 15, '91
Cover: What Do Media Buyers Think Of Radio Salespeople?
Interview: Richard Balsbaugh

#53 Jul. 29, '91
Cover: Pilgrimage To Arbitron
Interview: Frank Scott

#54 Aug. 12, '91
Cover: Where Does Your Motivation Come From?
Interview: Rush Limbaugh

#55 Sep. 23, '91
Cover: Building A Competitive Advantage
Interview: Jacqui Rossinsky

#56 Oct. 7, '91
Cover: Direct Marketing For Radio
Interview: Warren Potash

#57 Oct. 21, '91
Cover: DAB: How Will it Affect Us?
Interview: Joe Field

#58 Nov. 4, '91
Cover: 24-Hour Formats
Interview: David Rogers

#59 Nov. 18, '91
Cover: How To Solve Your Biggest Sales Problem
Interview: Robert F. Callahan

#60 Dec. 2, '91
Cover: Sales & Management Consultants
Interview: Carl C. Brazell Jr.

#61 Dec. 16, '91
Cover: The Year In Review
Interview: '91 Interview Review

#62 Jan. 6, '92
Cover: The History Of Group W Radio
Interview: Jim Thompson

#63 Jan. 20, '92
Cover: How To Write Great Radio Spots
Interview: James H. Quello

#64 Feb. 3, '92
Cover: Breaking The 6.8 Barrier
Interview: Gary Fries

#65 Feb. 17, '92
Cover: How To Sell Retailers
Interview: Bill Livek & Bill Engel

#66 Mar. 2, '92
Cover: Country Radio
Interview: Jerry Lee

#67 Mar. 16, '92
Cover: Hit Promotional Items
Interview: Steve Marx
Interview: Pierre Bouvard

#68 Mar. 30, '92
Cover: New Technology
Interview: Neil S. Robinson

#69 Apr. 13, '92
Cover: LMAs
Interview: Barry Umansky

#70 Apr. 27, '92
Cover: Collection Strategies
Interview: John Dille

#71 May 11, '92
Cover: Computerization Of Radio
Interview: Gary Stevens

#72 Jun. 8, '92
Cover: NAB Radio Montreux
Interview: Dick Clark
Interview: Nick Verbitsky

#74 Jun. 22, '92
Cover: Choosing Programming Consultants
Interview: Gordon Hastings

(Back issues prior to Aug. 10, '92 are Pulse of Radio issues. Offer based on availability.)

TO ORDER BACK ISSUES: CALL 1-800-226-7857

#75 Aug. 10, '92
Cover: AM Survival Strategies
Interview: David Kantor

#76 Nov. 2, '92
Cover: Radio Revenues
Interview: Jimmy de Castro

#77 Dec. 14, '92
Cover: The Year In Review
Interview: The Best Of '92 Interviews

#78 Jan. 4, '93
Cover: Short-Form Programming
Interview: Gary Fries

#79 Mar. 1, '93
Cover: Country Radio
Interview: Ken Greenwood

#80 Mar. 29, '93
Cover: Sports Radio
Interview: Paul Fiddick

#81 Jun. 7, '93
Cover: The Future of Formats
Interview: Bob Sillerman

#82 Jul. 12, '93
Cover: Making The Move From PD To GM
Interview: G. Gordon Liddy

#83 Aug. 9, '93
Cover: Increase Sales With Software
Interview: Bob Fox

#84 Aug. 23, '93
Cover: Traffic & Billing Automation
Interview: Dan Mason

#85 Sep. 6, '93
Cover: Great Copy on a Limited Budget
Interview: George Carlin

#86 Oct. 4, '93
Cover: The Marketing of Urban/Black Radio
Interview: Steve Morris

#87 Nov. 1, '93
Cover: Selling Cost Per Point
Interview: Gordon Hastings

#88 Nov. 15, '93
Cover: New Technology Review
Interview: Wayne Vriesman

#89 January 3, '94
Interview: Mel Karmazin

#90 Jan. 17, '94
Cover: Talk Radio
Interview: Hank Stram & Jack Buck

#91 Jan. 31, '94
Cover: Spanish Language Radio
Interview: Cary Simpson

#92 Feb. 14, '94
Cover: The Ultimate Sales Manager
Interview: Ralph Guild

#93 Feb. 28, '94
Cover: Marketing Country Radio
Interview: Frances Preston

HOW TO ORDER:

Within the U.S. and Canada, call 1-800-226-7857 or 407-655-8778 with your credit card information between 9 a.m. and 5 p.m. Eastern time.
Outside the U.S., call 407-655-8778.

To order by FAX:

Fax form with your credit card information and signature to 407-655-6164.

To Order by Mail:

Mail this form with your check or credit card information to:
Streamline Publishing, Inc., 224 Datura Street, Suite 718
West Palm Beach, Florida 33401-9601, U.S.A.

MAIL OR FAX ORDER FORM:

☐ Please enter my subscription to *Radio Ink* magazine, published every other week (25 times a year). The cost is $125.00 ($199 International.)

☐ Please send me ______ copies of *THE RADIO BOOK™: The Complete Station Operations Manual* (a three-book set) for $89.00 for all three (plus S&H and tax where required). I understand that if I am not satisfied with any book for any reason, I may return it within 30 days.

$89.95 each set $________

Fla residents add sales tax (6%) $________

Shipping & Handling $________

($5.50 per set in U.S. Overseas surface shipping add $10.00 per set. For Air Service to Alaska, Hawaii, Canada, Mexico and Central America, add $22.00 to book amount. For Air Service to all other foreign countries, add $32.00.)

TOTAL $________

Name/Title ________________________________

Station/Company ________________________________

Billing Address ________________________________

City/State/Zip ________________________________

Phone/Fax ________________________________

Shipping Address ________________________________

Checks to: Streamline Publishing, Inc. Amount enclosed $________.

Charge it to: ☐ MC ☐ VISA ☐ AMEX

Card # Exp. Date ________________________________

Signature ________________________________